MW01108362

Your Guide to Financial Freedom

Grow it.
Keep it.
Protect it.

Brett Machtig

Foreword by Ted Charles

Your Guide to Financial Freedom

Grow it. Keep it. Protect it.

MGI, LLC * Minneapolis * 2010
Revised 2016

Dedicated to reducing your tuition at the most expensive school there is...

The School of Hard Knocks

FOREWORD

By Ted Charles

I am a family man. I have a supportive wife, Jan and two daughters, Alli and Mandy. Over the years I went from a lowly salesperson to the Chairman and CEO of a major investment company.

At one point of my life, I had my girls making sales kits in our living room. "You'd be surprised about how painful a paper cut can be," says Alli, relating to her upbringing. "My Dad made us work– and hard."

Mandy related a story as to how she named her pet gerbil "Ted" after her dad because of his long family absences due to his work. And as I swaggered in after a hard day of at the office, all the family would be asleep – except for me, and the other "Ted" the gerbil who would be running like mad on the spinning wheel in his cage.

That night it hit me–I was not only Ted, the hard-working salesman coming home to his family, but I was also like "Ted" the gerbil on the spinning wheel– running with all my might–but getting nowhere.

I learned several lessons from "Ted," the gerbil. I learned (1) running keeps you fit and healthy as he lived for more than eight years, and (2) I do not want to be running on the financial treadmill, getting nowhere for my whole life.

I needed to create a plan to get off of this real-life spinning wheel. So the real Ted sought out a mentor who helped "Ted" become truly wealthy. In 1992 we started the now very successful broker dealer with almost $7 billion in assets under management in a publically traded company – Investors Capital (ICH).

I met Brett several years ago and he was one of our advisors. Since he had a great deal of experience consulting to Fortune 500 companies, we hired him to improve Investors Capital. The plan took Brett nine months to complete and we became very close.

While going over our plan at Donatello Restaurant in Lynnfield Mass. one autumn evening, I asked Brett an important question, "Why are you not one of our top advisors?"

He answered, while his corporate consulting practice was his primary income, he would make it a goal to become one of the firm's top advisors.

Unlike many of the visionaries I've met, Brett did exactly what he said he would do and significantly helped our company grow. Within two years, Brett became one of our top advisors. He has practical experience in the field in which he consults and does what he says he will do.

That is why I wanted to write the introduction to his book. If you follow the advice contained in these pages, you will be able to improve your financial condition. Two years after his consultation, our company has doubled its sales and value, partly due to Brett's recommendations and mostly due to the efforts of our company's team following the plan. Listen to him and you'll be glad you did.

This book is an attempt to make a difference in *your* life, so that money alone is not your driving factor. Reading and contributing to this book has made a difference in my life. Read it and do the financial checklist items in the back of the book Brett recommends. Enjoy the journey.

Like Forrest Gump said in the movie by the name, as he was explaining his fortune to the lady at the bus stop, "Being rich gave me one less thing to worry about."

Let this book be your guide to having one less thing to worry about.

Ted Charles
Chairman and Founder
Investors Capital Corporation

CONTENTS

INTRODUCTION

I'm so tired of working hard and making no progress on my financial plan. I get ahead, and then wham! We have some reversal that puts me off track, for the 10th time. Now instead of being older and wiser, I am just older. And I am running out of time. My 401(k) is now a 201(k).

I have saved some, but far from enough to ever support my lifestyle. I know I need to make changes, but I do not know what to change. I do not have time to make any more mistakes.

Does this sound like you? Doing O.K. but definitely not where you want to be? Well this book may be for you.

Believe it or not financial problems can be addressed within these pages.

We will break it down:
• Identify false ideas that keep you from saving

• Clarify how to invest so you make better returns

• Fix holes in your financial boat that you may not even know exist

• Save you from drowning in information so you can know exactly what to do, even in troubled economic times

Each chapter will address a different, but essential step in the wealth creation process. First we deal with why you are stressed about money and show you how to get rid of that stress right away. Then we teach you the most important thing about wealth—without addressing this one thing, wealth will NEVER come your way.

Then we get into the nitty-gritty about the five keys to successful investing. Believe me, without a clear understanding of these keys, investing will seem arbitrary and random. With the keys, your chance of success will be stacked in your favor.

Then we cover how to diversify, garner real tax savings, and demonstrate how to trim your risk so the next emergency does not set you back 10 more years, of which, you do not have.

And lastly, we will address how to pass on your wealth without giving it all to your needy uncle–Uncle Sam, and creating jealousy and marital problems for your kids–just because you were successful and died.

Can it be done in this short book? The answer is YES!

And when you are done reading this book, you can create a plan to set your boat off to sea to the future destination of your dreams–wealth, security, freedom, control, and with a little luck a sense of peace.

Each chapter will lead off with real-life stories to illustrate why it is important and how it can help you. Some will relate to you and some will not. Go with it. And by the end, it will become clear as to why it is important to create, retain, and protect financial freedom. You will know how to thrive when others are struggling even in poor economic times.

Why listen to Brett Machtig?

With 25 years of experience helping investors just like you, you are sure to find his stories and insights interesting and accurate.

This is not his first attempt to write a book.

In 1996, he wrote a book, *Wealth In A Decade*, which has helped tens of thousands of people learn how to get out of debt and have hope for a better life. Its message is as true today as when it was first published. You can go from debt to financial freedom in 10 years with the right guidance.

In 1999, he wrote a book to help businesses make more money. Specifically, the book identified the essential steps to improving long-term value for their owners or shareholders.

In these last 25 years retirees, school teachers, business owners, professionals, financial advisors, executives, and the newly rich have come to Brett for help. Brett has seen virtually every financial related problem, and has come up with a solution that is easy to understand and simple to implement.

Your Guide to Financial Freedom has simple goals. It will help you get it, keep it and protect it. Of course, by "it" I mean financial freedom.

Good luck on your journey to freedom,

Brett Machtig

Do not be unhappy if you are not where you want to be, particularly if you do not have a plan. Without a map, the chance of finding a particular destination is equally unlikely.

I. THE SECRETS TO BEING FINANCIALLY STRESS-FREE RIGHT NOW

*M*y cell phone rang as I was heading out of my Sandestin, Fla., office. I answered and it was Bill. "Brett, it's Bill. Can we meet for a drink?"

I told Bill I could meet him the following week at the Osaka Japanese Restaurant on Highway 98 in Destin, Florida. Bill answered, "That'll work," followed by a familiar click and he was gone.

That was just like Bill – a man of few words, in his sixties and with a long reputation of being able to fix anything. In our years working together, if I talked with Bill at all, it was at a dinner or at a planning session with his wife, Rita. He never said much, but when he did ask questions they showed insight and depth. I wondered what he wanted to talk about.

My answer came the following week. Bill was sitting at the restaurant with a half-full glass of beer in front of him. As I sat next to him, I could tell Bill was deeply troubled.

Bill turned to me and said, "I have bone cancer and the doctors give me six months to live."

The news stunned me.

Amazingly, Bill was less worried about his own health and concerns, and more worried about everyone else who would be affected.

"I just want to make sure I've planned properly and Rita has enough to live comfortably," he said.

I felt his unspoken pain, his love for his wife, and fear of the unknown all rolled into a ball in the pit of my stomach.

I told Bill that they stuck to their financial plan and their preparations over the years had already made it possible for Rita to live from the returns of their savings based upon their risk and return assumptions. Their asset goal had already become a reality. Bill said, "That is all I wanted to know."

About 30 minutes later, Rita joined us for dinner and we talked about how they met so many years ago because of a brand-new 1964 navy blue Ford Mustang convertible.

Rita added, "All I wanted was to ride in his cute sports car." That moment changed their lives forever and gave them each other for nearly half a century.

People turn to financial books for many different reasons, and with a wide range of personal circumstances.

You opened this book and are reading this page for a specific reason (or perhaps several reasons).

Perhaps:

- You have a fair amount of money saved, but it is in a money market account earning very little after taxes and inflation.
- Retirement is around the corner and you know you are not financially ready.
- You're retired and your investments are down significantly and you do not know what to do.
- You just went through a difficult divorce and are thrust into managing your own assets for the first time.
- You received significant money from selling your business and are afraid you'll lose it.
- You've already spent much more than intended from an inheritance and are afraid you'll spend the rest without guidance.

- You manage the family assets and you are searching for a trusted financial advisor as a backup, should something happen to you.
- The last time you updated your will was when your children were in diapers and they're now having children of their own. Back then, you had few assets and now your net worth is substantial–creating estate tax issues.
- You've bought this book for your spouse as a gentle hint to mutually get control of handle on your finances.
- You are an investment advisor who wants to find a way to bring complex financial issues down to simple concepts your clients can understand.
- You've realized managing assets requires knowledge, experience and time you lack and you're seeking some sort of help.

No matter the primary reason for reading this book, your first step is to create a financial plan.

You need to know where you are. Right now. Today. Throughout the book you'll see steps labeled ACTION ITEM. These are key steps you should consider when working through your own financial plan. Keep an eye out for these and work your way through them deliberately and carefully.

Consider reading this book to the end without taking every action step. Then, go through it again to answer the questions and action items throughout the book. In the back is a handy financial checklist so no financial stone is left unturned.

KNOW WHERE YOU ARE

Before you become a client of any wealth management firm, it's important to determine exactly where you are financially.

A reputable financial advisor will analyze your income, spending, cash flow, tax situation, debt structure, savings, retirement plans, insurance coverage, planned purchases and asset structure. This data can be secured through a personal interview, investment statements, debt balances and tax returns.

With this information in hand, your financial professional can assess where you have been in the past, financially. Together you can come up with some best estimates for how these aspects will change in the future.

While you may already know where you stand financially, the vast majority of people do not truly know their position. Simply working through this initial step is often an eye-opening experience, showing why a person is not as happy or secure about their finances as they would hope.

The majority of your work will most likely be on one or more of these lessons:

- Planning
- Cash flow
- Diversification
- Risk management
- Investment strategy
- Tax issues
- Estate planning
- Where to get help

Following are a few examples of people who once thought their situation was hopeless, but when focused on the creation of a plan to address one of the lessons above, discovered that they too could be financially free.

Jan was a stressed real estate broker in Panama City, Fla., who had trouble sleeping. She began our interview thinking she might need a little help, but felt she had things generally under control. Upon completing the plan, she realized she was in very poor financial shape – the root cause of her stress and sleep troubles. She realized if she did not act very quickly, she would run out of money within 18 to 24 months.

Together we focused on selling her real estate holdings which were consuming her liquid assets. Some of her real estate needed to be sold at a loss, and the equity that was left was added to her cash, paid off overwhelming debt and reduced her overall expenses.

Tom and Kim, a couple from southern Oregon "tried" to save while one of them piled on debt to start up a business. They fought often, over – you guessed it – money. Our meeting showed them the importance of creating a plan to light the way toward recovery from their debt and then move forward as a team.

Upon the creation of his plan, Al, a senior manufacturing executive from Boston, Mass., clearly saw he was getting further away from his goal of retirement. With each increase in his income, he offset the surplus with an even larger increase in spending. The net result was mounting debt and diminished annual savings. He said he felt depressed about being a slave to his lifestyle. We helped change the negative cash flow by using the plan to track increases and decreases of his cash flow. Within 30 months, this high earner and higher spender paid off all debt, except for his home mortgage. Finally, he got off the debt cycle and was progressing to financial freedom.

Andrew and Therese, a retired couple from Bloomington, Minn., realized after creating a plan that their investments were not growing, except when they added money to their account. We helped change their asset mix, investment strategy and set up performance measures so they knew whether their investments were on track or not.

Each of these situations was improved by creating a workable financial plan. Don't stop there. Set up a personal advisory team with a trusted financial advisor, a knowledgeable insurance specialist, a sharp accountant, a seasoned attorney and, if you run a business, an experienced business mentor who understands how to succeed in your business. This group will work much like a board of directors to help make sure your plan will succeed.

By clearly defining where you are right now, your advisory team can help you address roadblocks and quickly correct your course anytime you move away from your intended goals. Put this in writing and revise it at least quarterly.

The next step is to know where you want to go.

KNOW WHERE YOU WANT TO GO

Planning a compelling future is a relatively new option. Just a few centuries ago, your life would have been pre-determined by your family and social status. If your family came from a long line of butchers, most likely, that would be your future as well. If your family farmed, that would most likely be your lot in life. Conditions changed very slowly over the days, months, years and generations.

Today, your actions can significantly change your socio-economic future in a relatively short period of time. Your past does not have to equal your future. Having a plan in place is the key to making this socio-economic change happen. Otherwise you will be carried by the inertia of the financial decisions of your past.

Once you know where you are now, the next step is to figure out where you want to go. Write the story of your future life – as if it has already happened. Be sure to add in all the rich details to make this vision real for you.

Creating a plan and deciding where you want to go will give you "cause and control" over your future like no other action. It will help you keep your perspective in spite of minor setbacks. Creating and then following a plan will help bring about happiness and peace because you'll be more in control of your destiny.

Put it all into the story of your future life. Keep the size manageable and the journal handy so you can work on it while you are between meetings, at the cabin, or before you go to bed at night. We suggest keeping your plan in a 5" X 8" journal found in most any bookstore.

Start out your plan with the end in mind and work backwards. First, you'll want to create a 10-year vision, then one for five years, one for three years, and finally a one-year vision.

10-Year Vision

Write the story of your life as you see it in 10 years—as if it has already happened. Add in all the details to make this story or vision real for you. Visualize an average day in your life exactly 10 years from now.

Ask yourself, "What milestones will show that I have reached my goal?" "Where do I want to be?" "What roadblocks did I have to overcome or bad habits did I need to break?" "What are the non-financial goals I want to achieve?" Write your answers down to firmly set them in your mind.

Here are some more questions to ask yourself but make up your own questions as well:

- When do I want to retire?
- When do I want to be debt-free?
- How will we pay for our children's college?
- Do I want to move to a new home?
- What do I want to have, do or be in ten years?
- How can we meet our goals and still enjoy the ride?

Here are some non-financial keys to address in your vision.

➢ **Who are you with?** Who do you love and who loves you? What positive people and things do you want to have in your life? What toxic or negative people, influences and environments need to be eliminated to make the 10-year vision compelling for you?

➢ **How can you better serve others**? Serving others is a critical key to being successful and feeling good about it. Ask yourself, "What groups need my help?" "What do I have to offer?" "How can I better serve my children, family or spouse?" "Who can I help or mentor?"

➢ **Have you discovered your "Special Purpose?"** If you love what you do and are very good at it, you probably have already discovered your "special purpose." But if you do not love what you do, find that one thing–and focus your energies on excelling in that specialization. Not only will you be happier, you will be more successful.

➢ **Does your spouse "buy" the plan?** If you are married or have a partner, be sure the vision reflects both of your desires, directions and goals. Go to dinner or take a weekend trip and create compelling 10-year visions that excite *both* of you. Interview each other. Do not stifle the other's vision. Keep the discussion light and in the spirit of possibility. If your spouse truly isn't interested in planning, create the vision alone. Remember, the one who has the clearest vision will drive the family direction.

➢ **Include all planned purchases and when you plan to make them.** For example, let's say you are going to spend $15,000 to remodel your kitchen two years from now, replace your car three years from now, pay for four years of Susie's college beginning five years from now, and buy a cabin or second home in nine years. Put these planned expenses in your vision as well.

➢ **Does your plan need alterations?** Your 10-year vision may include staying in your current house until the kids leave or only replacing your cars every six years to build up your savings. It may even involve downsizing to live within your means, get out of debt and live a more stress-free life. You may be telling yourself, I don't want to live scrimping and pinching pennies. On the same note, ask yourself: do I want to be in the same place I am now ten years from now?

➢ If you plan to make more money, how will you do it? Include what you'll do to improve the economic value to your company. What training can you undertake? What skills need to be improved? What certifications should you get? When are you going to do these things? Who can mentor you?

➢ Address all the areas that have sabotaged your plans in the past. If you had a bad business partner, write out the lessons you learned from the experience. If you spent too much and were in financial trouble, write down what you did wrong, so you do not repeat past mistakes. For example, if over spending was caused by remodeling your home, write down what you have learned and what you can do to avoid repeating similar mistakes. If you have a friend or associate who has successfully handled the same problem, ask them how they overcame it and then model their behavior.

After you've crystallized your vision in writing of where you are now and created a compelling vision of where you want to be in 10 years, work backwards from the 10 year vision, bridging the future back to your present situation.

Action Item: Write down your 10-year visions. Include as many details as you possibly can.

Five-Year Vision

Now, figure out what you need to do, be, or have in five years to be on track for your 10-year vision. Be as specific as you can. Remember, the clearer your future vision, the more likely it will happen and the more likely you'll know if you are off-track.

After adding up all future expenses and planned purchases, is there enough money going into savings? Are you realistic about your income increases? Does your past support your future view or make it seem unlikely? In other words, if you spent more than you made over the last five years, what are you going to do differently so you can save this year? Remember, experience is important and mistakes are inevitable, but learn from these mistakes, do not repeat them.

As Tony Robbins said in one of his seminars, *Date with Destiny* (which we highly recommend), "When people do well they tend to party. When they do poorly, they tend to ponder." Pondering is good, but set up a personal policy so as not to continually repeat past mistakes. Write down exactly what you will change to avoid the same problems again, then run your solution by someone who has that problem solved.

Write down your five-year plan of where you need to be, what you need to do and what you hope to have to ensure that your 10-year vision is real to you and feels achievable.

Do you feel good about your ten and five year future? If you do not, go back and rework your 10-year vision until you feel GREAT about it and cannot wait to make it happen.

> **Action Item:** Write down your five-year visions to make your five-year vision real to you.

Three-Year Vision

Once you create your five-year plan, do the same thing for a vision three years from now. Address income, expenses, career, education, savings, trips, lifestyle and any planned purchases to create a compelling, but realistic goal you can eagerly move toward. Throughout this plan, you should ensure that your savings are going up and/or your debt is going down. Doing so creates better and better cash flow.

If you don't check and recheck your savings and debt management status, money will most likely continue to create stress, not freedom. It's so simple to understand, but much more difficult to live. Still, the reduction in stress created from operating true to your plan is priceless. Spending more than you make creates a buildup of debt and/or a reduction of savings over time and a parallel increase in stress.

In our line of work we see far too many people depressed about life because they have no control over their spending and debt. I've seen some even turn to drugs or alcohol, effectively masking the pain, and doing nothing to address the underlying problem. Take control here and you will be amazed at how it completely changes your overall attitude toward life.

If spending is a problem, a simple way to start the stress reduction process is to focus on your five largest bills and come up with specific ways you are willing to reduce them. If you're like most people, your largest bills might include your home mortgage, income taxes, autos, business expenses, debt, travel, child support, random purchases, home remodeling/repairs, dining out and insurance.

Most people, unless focused on reducing their largest bills, cut out the little pleasures that make life enjoyable, like going on a date with their spouse, having a cup of coffee at Starbucks or belonging to a health club. The results from cutting out the fun stuff usually are the same as going on a starvation diet; you don't lose weight and over the long run, you just get heavier (or in the case of money, more in debt).

Instead, for each major expense, come up with at least five ways to reduce it. Then, as a couple, decide on realistic savings ideas you'll truly implement to save at least 10 percent of every income dollar.

Write down your three-year vision of where you need to be in order to be on track for your five-year plan. Reread what you wrote for your five and 10 year vision to see if they are all aligned and compelling so you are excited about your future.

Does your future require you to spend less? Put in milestones that do not cost a lot, but may give lots of happiness like learning to play the guitar, going with a church group to help the poor, writing a novel, or doing a bike trip down the Pacific Coast with a good friend.

Action Item: Write down your three-year visions to make your three-year vision real to you.

Within One Year.....

Now, write a story of your "ideal scene" one year from now. Describe the milestones required to be on track. Depict how you will feel at that point, being on track towards your longer term plans.

Does your list of one-year goals in the plan look familiar? If it resembles your New Year's Eve resolutions from years past, ask yourself what you are willing to do differently to make them really happen. Write down what you want, why you want it and what you are willing to do to make it all happen.

Are you drifting away from your spouse? Come up with specific ways you can become closer. Have you addressed ways to improve your health? Come up with steps to eat better, exercise more or be more active. These may seem unrelated to the topic of money, until you consider the costs of divorce and being too ill to enjoy your wealth.

Finally, figure out what five things you need to do right now in order to move towards your one-year ideal scene. If there are decisions you have been putting off, decide which path is best for

Action Item: Write down your one-year vision, and more importantly, contemplate what five things you can do right now to help you step towards your ultimate destination.

you right now. This will give you a direction to go so you can focus your efforts. Get the balls rolling by putting on the list reading this book, and then doing all of the exercises, and committing them in writing to your journal.

Now, keep the plan current by reviewing and revising your plan at least quarterly. You're now on a three-month tracking program. It's not just manageable, it is achievable! Write your refinements in your journal every 90 days. Then, once a year, buy a new journal and revise and update your plan.

Remember the acid test for wealth accumulation: Are you going in the direction of your goals? Are you on track? Are you saving? Are you paying off debt? If the answer to any of these is, "No," consider getting help from a professional financial advisor.

Find Mentors

Do some leg-work to secure mentors who can help you avoid learning from the school of hard knocks. Remember: only when a student is ready does the teacher appear. Be on the lookout for your next teacher. In some cases, mentors may even have the power to increase your income and help move your plan along.

Write down what your mentors suggest to you and ask them to review your plan to see if you missed any key steps. Ask permission to check in with them from time to time to keep on track. You will find most successful people want to help others, as long as you maintain responsibility for following the advice and producing the results.

Find mentors who have mastered a particular area in which you need improvement. If they haven't done it themselves, they might lead you in the wrong direction. Interview them. Ask them how they did it. Write down what you learn. Go over your revised plan with your mentors to make sure you heard them correctly. Then, do what they suggest. Let them know what worked. Also, let them know what didn't work, as they might know how you can get back on track.

Action Item: Find mentors who can help you get results. List several mentors in your journal and when you will ask them if they can help. Interview them. Write up your revised plan, then go over what you heard from the mentor, based on their feedback.

WHAT NEEDS TO BE IN THE FINANCIAL PLAN?

To help you grow, keep and protect your money, so that you can live from its returns, several key terms need to be defined:

Net Income

What is your net income? Net income, is what you get to spend after taxes, after payroll deductions, after business expenses, and after alimony or child support, or after retirement contributions. It is your net paycheck.

You can improve net income by increasing your earned income. Ask yourself, "How can I improve my income by increasing my value to my company, to my co-workers, or to my customers? Far too many people simply expect more money without adding any more value. This almost never works, except for an inflationary wage increase or if it is early in a person's career.

More likely, if you do not add more value, you should plan for an eventual pay cut. Why? Well, as the United States becomes a smaller player in the global economy, somewhere in this world, someone is willing to do what you do for less money. Write in your journal how you can do your job better for your clients and colleagues.

Your best defense against a pay cut is to continually strive to do your job better. Or consider going into a more lucrative line of work. Educate yourself or interview someone already getting the financial results you want in your field, or outside of it.

Taxes

It is possible to reduce your taxes or payroll deductions. There are many ways of doing it, from starting a business to giving away the "junk" in your attic. In the chapter on tax planning we'll explore how to find a good accountant and where to look for the best deductions before the year is over.

List some ways you can reduce your taxes. See the chapter on The Real Keys To Tax Reduction for ideas.

Payroll Deductions

Payroll deductions include many that you cannot change like FICA, FUTA, Medicare and withholdings. They also include deductions you can change, like your 401(k)s, 403(b)s and TSAs – your pre-tax retirement contributions.

Consider setting your 401(k) or retirement savings percent at least to the amount your employer matches. For example, if your employer matches the first five percent, set your minimum 401(k) contribution to five percent. Anything above that depends on your cash flow and savings discipline.

If you tend to spend everything you get your hands on – max out your retirement contributions. If you are a good saver, however, consider diverting non-matched retirement contributions to debt reduction to improve your cash flow. Most families can reduce their spending by 25-50% by doing this.

Try to estimate what your net income will be for the next 10 years and outline your plan to increase your net income. If you don't know, guess. You are the only person who has to believe in the plan 100 percent for it to work. Be conservative on your income guesses and err on the side of under-estimating your income. If you have been getting inflationary wage increases and believe they will continue, add an inflation increase to both income and expenses.

Here is a sample plan to show you how to create a for your income, debt-payoff, expenses and savings.

To illustrate, *if Pete, an electrician, increased his debt by $25,000 over the year but his savings stayed the same, he has worsened his financial condition by spending $25,000 more than he makes.*

If your savings went up and/or debt went down then you are spending less by that amount.

For example, *35-year-old Anne has $20,000 more in her checking account and $30,000 less debt over the course of a year. That means Anne spent $50,000 less than her net income of $100,000. This is good. Anne is saving 50 percent of her net income.*

If you own rental property, track all the costs of continuing property ownership such as property taxes, repairs, insurance, rental fees, etc. Then, compare your rental income to your rental property expenses. Do not add in property appreciation for now.

Are you making any money? What is your annual return? To find this, divide the net property income excluding property appreciation by your net equity.

If you were to sell it and pay off your debts, how would this improve your cash flow and debt reduction? If you earn less than five percent on the investment property excluding appreciation, consider selling the property. As in the earlier example, if you own a rental property that costs you more than you receive in income, sell it and use your equity to pay off debts. If there is no equity, consider selling it anyways to reduce your monthly outflow.

The biggest mistake we see in property ownership is not having the discipline to know when to buy and when to sell. For example, we only buy if we can net 10 percent positive cash flow excluding appreciation. We do not build in any appreciation into a "buy" decision. We also will only buy at a discount to the true value of the property, so if we need to sell, we can without a loss.

If it does appreciate or rents drop so cash flow is five percent or less, we sell. Consider using these standards for all your investment real estate.

By using this example, you can create a financial plan for yourself. Upon creating this plan you will know where you are and where you want to go! What else is necessary to stay on track? The answer lies where the rubber meets the road – living out the plan, reviewing your results and making adjustments along the way to achieve your goals.

MONITOR AND ADJUST TO STAY ON TRACK

It is simply not enough to create a great plan. You have to keep it current and updated. The plan must be taken out and reviewed at least quarterly. If you are off track, revise your actions toward what it takes to achieve your goals.

You're heading in the right direction if you see:

- Gross income increasing
- Net income increasing
- Expenses decreasing
- Debt balances decreasing
- Annual savings increasing
- Portfolio value increasing

You're moving away from your goals if you see:

- Debt increasing
- Debt payments increasing
- Savings decreasing
- Expenses increasing
- Net income decreasing
- Portfolio value decreasing

Don't expect perfection right away. Getting on track and staying there is a continually evolving process. When a plane flies from New York to London it is off-track most of the flight as weather and winds change its course. With each change, the pilot and the plane's computers retarget the plane to its destination until it is ultimately reached in the end. Many of life's roadblocks, like weather and wind, exist to keep your plan from becoming a reality. The rest of this book addresses key issues and how you can stay on track and reach your destination.

Financial success is that simple. The secret to stress reduction, relating to your finances, is having a plan and then following it.

You can take a simple test and prove it to yourself.

Step 1 – Rate your financial stress from a low of 1 to a high of 10.
Step 2 – Create a financial plan and begin to follow it.
Step 3 – Retest your financial stress.

Remember Bill from the beginning of this chapter? Well, about two weeks before Bill's death, his wife, Rita called, asking me to come down to Florida.

When I arrived at Bill's hospital room, I didn't know what condition to expect Bill in. To my surprise and delight, Bill was mentally sharp and without complaint, even though we sensed he was in great pain.

A few days later, Bill passed away with his beloved Rita at his side. The church was packed for his funeral. I looked over the church and was amazed at how many people had been touched by Bill in some way.

We knew Bill was at peace knowing Rita was financially free and following their plan, the one they created together.

In the next chapter we will address the single most important factor in achieving your financial success, but first here is the chapter summary.

SUMMARY

1. Know where you are by taking a realistic snapshot of your financial situation. Establish where you are now financially by using the examples in this chapter as a guide.

2. Start with the end in mind. Create a compelling future 10 years out. Once that 10-year vision is clear, work backwards to create a plan for five years, three years and one year. Then, identify five things you need to do *right now* to be on track.

3. Test your financial stress before and after creating your plan. If it gives you a feeling of cause and control over your finances, your stress level will drop. If not, refine your plan until you believe it will work.

4. Pull out your plan and check to see if you are on track at least quarterly. Adjust your course to stay or get on track.

5. Find mentors who have already achieved the goals you seek. Have them check the validity of your plan and point out shortfalls. Build an advisory team of your mentors, a trusted financial advisor, tax advisor and attorney to serve as your "board of directors" to help you stay on track.

6. If you need help creating your plan, see an experienced financial advisor. Another option is to contact our office for a free spreadsheet to track your cash flow and creating a plan.

the secrets to being financially stress-free

By reading and addressing what is taught in this chapter, financial freedom is possible. Without it, you have no chance at all.

II. THE SINGLE MOST IMPORTANT FACTOR TO FINANCIAL SUCCESS

*K*en is a husband, father of two healthy kids and a senior programming specialist for a software company. He lives outside of Fort Lee, New Jersey in a sleepy bedroom community just outside of New York City. Before we met Ken, the company he worked for was purchased by a publicly-traded international software company. In addition to Ken's wages, he had received stock options for almost 10 years prior. When the company was sold, the stock options were worth $2 million after taxes.*

Ken was referred to us by another client who also worked for the same company. Based upon the data collected, we created his plan.

Before the windfall, Ken and his wife, Margaret were doing quite well. Ken earned $100,000 in net income and saved almost $25,000 per year. They had saved about $250,000 in their IRAs, excluding his stock options. They owed about $385,000 between their car loans, mortgage and a second mortgage that had grown over time.

We suggested using the windfall to become debt-free and create enough passive income so they could live off their portfolio instead of wages. Ken had missed much of their kids' lives as a hi-tech executive and now he would finally have a chance to enjoy his family. After paying off their debt, they would have enough assets to get a 50-percent pay increase without ever having to work again, assuming an 8% return on investment (results not guaranteed).

Ken listened to our suggestions, but had other plans for his windfall.

He let us manage his $250,000 IRA and began building a dream house for his family in Tarrytown, New York. He planned to increase the "investment" in their home from $600,000 to $2.4 million. He felt all his hard work had finally paid off. He could at last give his family the better things in life. The dream house quickly became a nightmare as it took longer and cost more than anticipated, with almost $450,000 in cost overruns.

At the very least, Ken could have kept his mortgage balance low on the new home. But, after talking to his mortgage broker, he decided to borrow 90 percent of the home's value with "cheap money," then used the remaining cash to put down payments on several investment real estate properties to parlay his small fortune into a large one.

Ken and his wife soon upgraded their furniture, cars, private schools and just about everything else. Without any wage increases, Ken's personal expenses went from just $75,000 per year pre-windfall to $225,000 annually post-windfall.

In no time, Ken owned several "cannot lose investment" properties, with all their associated mortgages, property taxes, insurances and repairs. His real estate broker assured him he would make money on the appreciation of his investment property. Ken's future wealth "hummed and glowed" in his mind. Margaret didn't understand high finance but she had a bad feeling about it all. The property's carrying costs added another $225,000 per year above any rental income and on top of his personal expenses of another $225,000.

Now, with only $100,000 coming in and $450,000 going out, the cash was going down very quickly, in spite of a vast net worth.

Have you ever wondered how rock stars or lottery winners or trust fund babies can lose it all, even though they have enough wealth to buy a small country? The answer lies in cash flow. Or better stated – the answer lies in the lack of cash flow.

THE IDEAL CASH FLOW

What is cash flow? It is the amount of money you have after paying all your bills and purchases.

If you spend more than you make, there are symptoms: you have no cash, a high level of financial stress, and lots of increasing debt. You are in a negative cash flow position; more money is going out than coming in.

If you spend less than you make there are symptoms as well. You have savings, you are reducing debt, you have a positive financial outlook. This is a positive cash flow state – more money is coming in than going out.

Ideal cash flow is having enough non-retirement savings so you can live from your investment portfolio income within a reasonable time. For the purposes of this book, ideal minimum positive cash flow is at least 10 percent of funds that are free to use, save or pay-off debt after paying all expenses and all purchases. For the purposes of this chapter, savings does not include savings into your retirement accounts, since they do not impact your daily cash flow and have limited access without adverse tax consequences.

Without good cash flow, the chances of accumulating enough money to live off your investments are slim to none. That is why we put so much emphasis on this topic. Improving your cash flow should be your number one priority. It truly is that important to ensuring your financial freedom.

Like Ken and Margaret, the lesson of cash flow is usually learned from pain rather than discipline. Some people learn its importance from a job loss, cash-draining investment choices, health problems, economic downturns, or needy adult kids. Many people, unfortunately, never learn its importance and continue to struggle financially.

As you read this chapter today, where are you in terms of cash flow?

- Do you have GREAT cash flow? We define GREAT cash flow as saving 50 percent or more of every dollar you make in net income.

- Do you have GOOD cash flow? We define GOOD cash flow as saving 10 to 50 percent of net income.

- Do you have POOR cash flow? We define POOR cash flow as saving less than 10 percent of your net income.

If you're not happy with your cash flow, you can do something about it. Yes, it takes discipline and can involve some difficult choices, but in the long-term, getting a firm handle on cash flow is the best thing you can do for yourself and your family.

GREAT CASH FLOW – WHAT TO DO

If you are saving 50 percent or more of your net income – well done! Consider yourself amongst a small minority. You could stop here and skip on to the next chapter. However, with great cash flow already, I'm guessing you're driven to read on to improve things even more.

One small suggestion: Use that great cash flow to retire any remaining debt. Most likely you've already done so, but if not, this step will help you save even more down the road. Keep up the good work!

> **Action Item:** Write in your journal which cash flow condition best describes your situation: GREAT, GOOD or POOR. Follow the appropriate program below.

GOOD CASH FLOW - WHAT TO DO

If you are saving 10 to 50 percent of your net income, you may be well on your way to becoming wealthy. To make your position even better, use at least half of your monthly savings to clear up debts. This may seem obvious, but the following illustration will help drive home this point.

Suzy, the "Good Cash Flow" Example

Suzy, a 50-something flight attendant from Miami, Fla., is doing very well in spite of going through a difficult divorce. She earns $80,000 per year from a combination of wages and alimony.

As a flight attendant, Suzy has learned the importance of having a backup plan. Since she has already been through many financial struggles, countless industry lay-offs, pay cuts and corporate restructurings, as well as a divorce from a pilot who had too much fun on his international layovers. She has been preparing for a rainy day for a long time. In fact, she saves 20 percent of every paycheck. "I can only count on myself," says Suzy.

"So my financial future is in my own hands."

When we looked at Suzy's spending, her largest expense by far (like most Americans) was her debt payments. She owed $197,500 between her car, credit card and condo mortgage. Her total payments were $2,360 per month or $28,320 per year, or about half of her monthly expenses.

Without this debt burden her other monthly and annual expenses would have been $3,000 per month or $36,000 per year.

According to her plan, Suzy will pay $20,000 extra per year towards her debt, on top of her car, credit card, and mortgage payments of $28,320. As a result, by paying a total of $48,320 per year, she will be debt-free in four and a half years and earning enough from her investments to cover her current expenses in six years.

As you can see, by using at least half of your free cash flow you can begin to pay off your debt in a very short time. Use Suzy as an example. Write in your journal what you can do to pay off your consumer debt in no more than four years, and no more than 10 years for your mortgages. Paying off your debt will significantly increase your cash flow long term.

POOR CASH FLOW - WHAT TO DO

Are you saving less than 10 percent of your net income? Are you just keeping your head above water? Are you a slave to your lifestyle, increasing your debt or just consuming your net pay every year?

How do you get the cash flow engine started? From the above example, it is easy to see the impact of getting out of debt. But, if you are just barely paying the bills, you need to add one more step. You need to spend less on each of your five largest bills and increase your income.

So, how do you do it? Make a date with your significant other to address the situation. Get a babysitter for the kids, a bottle of wine and set aside the necessary time to truly look at where your extra spending is coming from. If you are divorced or single, sit down with a trusted advisor.

Are you eating out too often? Do you live in a home that is more than you can afford? Do you have expensive tastes in cars, clothes or travel? You need to figure out what you need to change right now so you can save an ideal 20 percent.

Why 20 percent? That way you do not have to spend your whole life stressed out and working. Also, it will make 10 percent in actual savings much more likely, because unexpected purchases, repairs, etc., can waylay the best of plans.

Let's look at ways to increase your income and review the top expenses and some possible solutions to cut costs.

Increase Your Income

What ways can you add more value to your employer to deserve more compensation. Here are some ways to increase your family's income:

- Have your spouse work

- Take on a part-time job

- Ask for a raise

- Set up a performance bonus

- Increase your output

- Move to a more prosperous area

- Do something else that pays more

- Get training, licensing or a degree

- Go into sales or into a professional field where the pay is higher

- Be mentored by successful people who earn more than you by working in the same field as you.

Action Item: Referring to your plan from the previous chapter, decide whether you want to increase your income, knowing at what cost it will be to you (time, more schooling, etc.). If you do, write down possible ways to increase family income.

Reduce Debt Expenses

Of all the expenses, debt pay-down is the major key to improving cash flow for most families. Here are some ways to reduce debt expenses:

- Set up a plan to pay all non-mortgage debt in four years or less
- Negotiate lower interest rates and lock in low fixed rates (avoid adjustable rates)
- Sell assets to pay off debts
- Consider using retirement assets to pay off debt
- Stop buying "stuff" until debt-free
- Cut up your credit cards and use cash exclusively
- Minimize business expenses, until debts are paid off
- Sell toys, stuff, etc., to pay off debt
- Develop your own creative ways to pay off debts

Reduce Business Expenses

In many cases, a business owner will spend money for the business when they would not spend that same money personally. Consider the following ways to reduce the business expenses:

Shut down or sell businesses consuming cash
- Save the first 20 percent of profit, then limit bills to the remaining 80 percent
- Clamp down on any unnecessary expenses
- Put systems in place to speed up cash payments into the business and make it hard to approve expenses
- Buy instead of leasing to avoid future payments
- Set a price ceiling for hotels, meals, etc.
- Use windfalls to pay off debt
- Provide incentives for cost-reduction ideas your company implements
- If business has limited income potential, sell where possible, or shut down and move on
- Buy used equipment instead new

- Bid out insurance, materials and professional services regularly
- Look at each product line – make sure each adds to the bottom line. If not, remove unprofitable lines
- Replace marginal employees quickly
- Promote, produce and advertise out of low income emergencies instead of borrowing

Action Item: If applicable to you, identify business expenses you can cut now and other expenses you can drop over the next 12 months.

Reduce Child-Related Expenses

By teaching your children how to save, you will not only reduce your expenses now, you will also make them feel self-sufficient and reduce your expenses in the future. Here are a few pointers:

- Pay for your children's needs, but have your children pay for their own wants
- Don't create a "welfare state" within the family by over-supporting or enabling a lifestyle your children cannot support
- Don't give children or teens credit cards
- Teach children to limit consumer spending to half of their income, while saving half
- Encourage kids to also save for college
- Give kids chores so they learn to be responsible
- Consider having kids take subsidized college classes while in high school to reduce college tuition expenses
- Put teens "in charge" of their expenses like insurance

Action Item: Identify and reduce unnecessary child-related expenses.

Reduce Vacation Expenses

Travel can be an expensive item for a family. Here are ways to keep costs down:

- Go on company-paid trips
- Go on tax-deductible trips with your church to help others where sponsorship is available
- Shop for travel bargains online at sites such as lastminute.com
- Set a budget and limit travel expenses to targeted amount
- Visit countries with favorable exchange rates
- Use frequent flyer miles

Action Item: Reduce travel expenses by having a budget and planning with these tips.

Reduce Insurance Expenses

Insurance can be a very high expense. Here are some ways to cut costs:

- Stay healthy: Work out, eat right and get enough rest
- Bid out life, health, disability, auto, long-term care and liability insurance regularly
- Create an insurance trust to reduce estate taxes
- Increase your deductibles to lower the policy cost as savings increase
- Have business pay for insurance, but know the tax consequences
- Maintain a good driving record
- Make fewer claims against your home and auto policies
- Don't smoke

> **Action Item:** Write down how you plan to reduce your insurance expenses.

Reduce Home Expenses

One of the largest expense items is your home. Look at ways to reduce these expenses:

- Use cash flow to pay mortgage sooner
- Convert variable-rate loans to fixed-rate loans
- Rent instead of owning a home if you plan on moving within five years
- Move to a smaller home
- Bid out insurance costs regularly
- Get your lender's permission to cancel mortgage insurance once loan is below 80 percent market value.
- Do not borrow more than 80 percent of your home's value
- Put off remodeling home
- Pay down mortgage with investments

> **Action Item:** Write down how you plan to reduce your home expenses.

Reduce the Cost of "Toys" and Second Homes

It is amazing what we spend on grown-up toys – boats, motorcycles, airplanes, RVs, etc. Here are a few ways to make those grown-up playthings cost less:

- Sell your toy
- Buy a less expensive toy

- Buy fractional interest in a toy
- Buy with a partner or family
- Put a toy into a business
- Have friends with toys
- If it floats, flies or sits most of the time unused, rent and don't buy
- Add up the total cost; figure cost per use; determine whether to own versus rent
- Transfer carrying costs to users
- Use www.craigslist.com to get toys cheap

Action Item: Make a list of toys you don't need any more, and what you plan to do with them now.

Reduce Auto Expenses

Automobiles can represent status as well as mere transportation. Consider these suggestions to reduce your vehicle expenses:

- Consider less expensive vehicles
- Consider an extended warranty to minimize car maintenance costs
- Bid out insurance costs regularly
- Rent cars for high mileage trips
- Sell cars that aren't getting used
- Donate unused cars to charity
- Get a car with better gas mileage
- Move closer to work
- Keep your cars longer
- Find the best deal online to help negotiate better pricing locally

Action Item: Write down how you plan to reduce your auto expenses.

Reduce Unplanned Expenses

Unplanned expenses can make up a major source of expenses. Here are some ways to minimize the costs:

- Carry fewer credit cards with lower limits, pay off monthly
- Limit access by paying yourself a weekly cash allowance to each spouse
- Never buy groceries if hungry
- Set a maximum limit you can spend without spousal approval
- Limit going where you spend – malls, QVC, eBay, Amazon.com, shopping vacations or shoe stores
- Task the most responsible and frugal spouse in charge of the checkbook, limit money access of the free-spending spouse

Action Item: Look at your expenses for the past 3 months and identify areas of excessive unplanned spending.

Reduce Remodeling Expenses

Remodeling can send a savings plan out the window. Here are some tips:

- Put off remodeling
- Check referrals of contractors before hiring
- Get multiple fixed bids for your remodeling projects
- Limit remodeling to projects that increase the resale value, like upgrading the bath, kitchen or curb appeal
- Do not pay the full balance of a bill until work is completed to your satisfaction
- Hire inspector to ensure work is done before paying final bill

- Buy materials from discount stores – Sam's Club, Costco, Amazon.com, ebay.com, directbuy.com, saveclub.com, craigslist.com

Action Item: Write down how you plan to reduce your remodeling expenses.

Reduce Investment Real Estate Expenses

Many investment property purchases do not make financial sense. Here are some ways to reduce your real estate expenses:

- Do not buy any real estate that cannot return 10 percent or more cash flow after all expenses, excluding appreciation
- If you cannot sell, lower your price, even sell at a loss if it still improves your overall monthly cash flow
- Transfer costs by selling as a "rent-to-own"
- Consider offering owner financing
- Rent property to contractor who can remodel in lieu of rent or for reduced rent
- Refinance variable mortgages to a fixed rate to prevent rate increases
- Sell a share of property to partner
- Donate property to charity. If the real estate pays less than 5 percent, consider selling it
- Transfer operating costs to renters
- Get lender to allow short sale A short sale is where a lender agrees to sell real estate for less than the loan balance

> **Action Item:** If applicable, evaluate your current real estate investments and identify places to save.

Now, go through the various expense lists and pick at least three things you will do to reduce your spending so that you can save a minimum of 20 percent. Yes 20%, because from experience, it takes more than just a 10% identified reduction to actually get the results of a 10% actual spending reduction.

Remember what we said at the beginning of the chapter, poor cash flow is why most people never save. Do not put this difficult step off or you will be in the same boat next year.

WHY MOST PEOPLE NEVER BECOME WEALTHY

Remember Ken and Margaret from the beginning of this chapter? They came to us once they recognized how bad their financial situation truly was.

We recommended they sell their home and other properties which did not add to their cash flow, even if it meant selling them at a loss. It took about 12 months, but they sold enough property which included their "dream" home to reduce their personal and business annual expenses from $450,000 per year down to $100,000.

They lost 75 percent of their windfall in two years. They learned an expensive lesson, but now they have a much better understanding of the importance of cash flow.

After their "dream house" sold they moved back to their old neighborhood in Fort Lee, New Jersey, in a slightly larger home. They still owe about $115,000 on their new home and have $100,000 in non-retirement funds after paying off their cars. They have their retirement fund which is worth $350,000. In two years, they plan on being debt-free.

This chapter will either be very easy or very hard for you. The pay-back for doing these exercises is life-changing, once you have done them long enough to build savings. Decide now that you will do what it takes to free up at least 10 percent of your net pay and use it to start eliminating your debt.

Use the ideas outlined in this chapter or make up your own to eliminate your debt through expense savings. Six months from now, you can expect to either be in the same place or you will begin to feel the freedom that a little cash flow can bring.

We have now covered what the single most important factor to financial success is: creating positive cash flow. Now, we are ready to address how to increase the investing success in your portfolio.

But first, let's review.

SUMMARY

1. Cash flow is the single most import factor as to whether you become financially free or become a slave to your lifestyle.

2. To change your cash flow, you must first analyze your income, taxes and spending.

3. Find out how much you currently save as a percent of your net income:

   - Your savings is GREAT if you are saving at least 50 percent of every dollar. Keep up the good work!

   - Your savings is GOOD if you are saving at least 10 to 50 percent of every net income dollar. Use your free cash flow to retire your debt in no more than four years. Every year you should retire 25 percent of your consumer debt and stop adding to the debt pile. Once your consumer debt is gone, use everything you were using to pay off debt, plus half of your free cash flow, to retire your mortgage in no more than 10 years. Before you know it, you'll have eliminated the average American family's largest expense – debt.

   - Your savings is POOR if you are saving less than 10 percent of your net income. You need to reduce your largest bills until you have a planned free cash flow of 20 percent. Then, follow the plan of GOOD savers for even less financial stress.

4. If getting started on reducing debt is overwhelming to you at this point in your life, be sure to connect with a trusted

financial advisor who can guide you through the process. Do not let yourself be too overwhelmed. Take control of the situation. You will be glad you did.

For most, investing is just a gamble. Given the choice of being a casino owner or a gambler, we suggest being the casino owner, because that way the odds are in your favor of making money. By learning how to improve your odds, saving becomes easier, success seems less arbitrary, and the short-term ups and downs become less stressful.

III. SIX KEYS TO HELP INCREASE YOUR INVESTING SUCCESS

I met Kim and Chet several years ago. Kim was very excited about life and her massage practice in Destin, Fla. She talked about her hopes and dreams with her husband, Chet.
"What brings you to Destin?" asked Kim.

I replied that I was there to meet with some long time clients of mine – Joe and Susan.

Joe and Susan asked us to help with their personal asset management about a decade ago. Joe wanted to start his own telecom contract consulting business. We helped him with his business using concepts from The Corporate Guide to Profit & Wealth.

About five years into our relationship, they moved to Destin. One day, as we walked along the white sugar beach together right after the move, Joe said, "Someday I will have a house on this beach!" A couple of times a year we met to update their strategic plans. Sure enough, Joe and Susan did build their dream house on that very same stretch of the beach we walked on years earlier.

Upon hearing about Joe and Susan, Kim asked us for help. Kim and Chet, meanwhile, had very mixed results in investing and *asked if we could help them, just as we helped Joe and Susan. They were very good savers but they did not understand what made a good investment. Eighty-percent of their net worth was in two stocks. One stock came from the sale of a family business and the other was their "dream stock." They decided to hire us and we helped them become not only great savers, but great investors by working with them to understand what makes for a great investment.*

So, what does make a great investment? And, how do you shift the odds in your favor to make money over time? This chapter will outline proven wealth strategies that will help you be "the casino owner" versus the gambler when it comes to your investments.

My own personal experience, as well as results of several well-known studies, shows investors do not do well without some type of professional help. One study conducted for the brokerage industry indicated investors working on their own make less than 4 percent on their investments.

We will cover six key concepts to help improve your investing success.

THE SIX KEY CONCEPTS TO INVESTING

Review the keys to investing so the odds are in your favor to make money, so that you become the casino owner instead of the gambler. There are, of course, other ways to invest and make money, but we will cover only those strategies we employ. Here are the five key investing concepts:

1) Understand what makes an "asset" an "investment"
2) Learn to buy at a bargain, sell when everyone wants "in"

3) Learn to make money after taxes and inflation
4) Learn to comfortably ride up and down markets as they "breathe"
5) Active Investing (Buy and Hold No Longer Works)

6)   The Key Factor to Making Money in Any Investment
      – The Selling Discipline

We will examine each of these key concepts in depth. The goal is that you become so familiar with these concepts that you apply them in your life with every investment decision you make.

Key Concept #1 – Understand What Makes an "Asset" an "Investment"

The ideal investment should make more sense now that we have covered some basic principles of individual wealth creation. As it turns out, the very same things that will improve your cash flow and financial condition are important considerations in good investment opportunities as well. Here are two very important clarifications you need to understand about your current holdings: The difference between an asset and an investment.

Assets: An asset is something you own of value. A car, a house, a college education, a business, an investment property, a doll collection, a cabin, cash, IRAs, 401(k), brokerage accounts, and your wedding ring all meet this broad definition. For the purposes of this book, an asset is something you own that you can sell for money.

Assets either cost you money or pay you money. We differentiate between these two types. If an asset costs you money to own, it is not an investment for the purposes of this book. In fact, the more assets you have that cost you money to own, the more investments you need to pay for them. To make it crystal clear as to how cost-increasing assets impact your cash, we will call them "non-producing assets." "Non-producing assets" cost you money. Non-producing assets are not necessarily bad. We all have many of them that we need and want. They make the "American Dream" worthwhile.

Here is a list of common non-producing assets that cost you money.

- Home
- Car
- Wedding ring
- Cabin
- Money-losing businesses

- Money-costing insurance
- Timeshare
- Art
- Boat
- Poor cash-flowing properties

Investments: Webster's dictionary defines an investment as, *"the investing of money or capital in order to gain profitable returns, as interest, or appreciation in value."* For the purposes of this book, an investment must be able to pay you money, now or sometime down the road.

Here is a list of common investments that can pay you money:

- Money market accounts
- Bank accounts
- Certificates of Deposit
- 401(k)s
- 403(b)s
- Collectables you sell for profit
- Stocks, mutual funds
- Most annuities

- Money-making life insurance
- Brokerage accounts
- Retirement accounts
- Bonds
- Good cash-flowing properties
- Contracts for deed
- Money-making Businesses

In short, an investment pays you money. If an asset costs money to own, it is NOT an investment, it is a "non-producing asset."

To determine if something is an investment, we look at its impact on you. If you have to pay your hard-earned net income to support the asset, it is not an investment for the purposes of this book. If it is paying you greenbacks, net income, capital gains, dividends,

Action Item: List your assets. Identify if they are non-producing or investments.

interest, spendable asset growth, or a cash flow that you can count on when you need it, it is an investment. This test alone determines whether or not your assets are investments. Let's look at some assets that many people consider "investments" and compare them to our definition to see if they qualify.

You will see the same asset can qualify as an investment for one family and not for another. The goal is to keep your "non-producing assets" that cost you money to a minimum while increasing your "investment assets" that can pay you money.

Your Home – Non-Producing Asset

Let's start with most Americans' largest asset–their home. Most people consider their home their most valuable investment. They rationalize buying a home much larger than they need so they can enjoy the use of their largest investment. They remodel their home constantly to increase its value.

But is owning a home an investment based upon our definition? Does your home pay you money or do you have to pay money to maintain it? After answering this question, most readers recognize that their home is a "non-producing asset" because the bigger it is the more it costs.

Also, you have to live somewhere and as you adjust into better, bigger and more expensive homes – it is unlikely you will capitalize on the home investment. More likely, your standard of living will simply increase. Can you turn your home into an investment? Of course you can. You can rent out part of your home so that part of the costs can be converted into an investment, as defined in this book. One widowed and retired client rents out a room to college students to keep herself company, and gets rental income as an extra perk.

Investment Property – Can Be Either A Non-Producing Asset or an Investment

So what about investment property? Is it an investment, based upon the definition of this book? The answer depends upon whether or not you receive enough cash to pay all expenses relating to the property and have enough left to call it an investment after you adjust for the income tax savings, mortgage interest, repairs, property taxes, vacancies, advertising, owner-paid utilities, insurance, and other direct costs, excluding appreciation. When you buy a property you will only buy in areas you believe will go up in value. We recommend you not put that appreciation in your decision to hold or buy, particularly if the property will cost you cash every month to keep it.

Unfortunately, we know many investors who have lost it all, filed for bankruptcy, were foreclosed upon, were stuck in a money-pit property they could not sell, or suffered a terrible financial setback just because they invested in a negative cash flow situation hoping for appreciation without the supporting cash flow.

Here is an example of a non-producing property losing two percent (-2%) annually:

Property Income:		
Rent	$18,000	$18,000
Property Expenses:		
Interest	($ 12,000)	
Property Taxes	($2,500)	
Insurance	($1,000)	
Utilities	($500)	
Repairs	($1,000)	
Association Dues	($3,000)	($ 20,000)
		($2,000)
Balance Sheet:		
Investment Property		$ 300,000
Mortgage		($200,000)
Investment Equity		$ 100,000

Negative Return on this "Non-producing Asset":   (2%)

In the above example, the investment property is a non-producing asset. If a lot or property has no revenue, it is never an investment by this book's definition. We do not include appreciation in our calculations, because so many people who have invested over the years expected to capitalize on appreciation, only to have lost market value and worse, could not recoup the money they put into it once they realized their cash flow mistake.

Therefore, your rental property is an investment only if it pays you enough rent to pay all related bills and you have enough cash left over to earn at least five percent on your equity. Investment equity is the market value of your property, less disposal costs, and the related consumer and mortgage debt. Can you turn your rental property into an investment, as defined by this book?

If you are losing cash now, you can improve your cash flow by:

- Lowering your cost structure
- Increasing your rent
- Taking on a partner
- Donating it to reduce taxes
- Selling with owner-financing
- Selling it outright
- Renting to own

By making the hard choices and making sure all investments pass the definition, as defined in this book, you will do well. Buy property that passes the cash flow tests or use the proceeds to pay down other debts. Then, you can use the proceeds from a poor cash flowing property, even if you sell it at a loss.

Business – Can Be Either A Non-Producing Asset or an Investment

Does your business pass the test? Does it pay you money or do you have to pay for the privilege of owning it?

Jodie is a long-time client who owns an eyewear and contact business in downtown Minneapolis. She had owned her shop for more than 20 years and had made enough money to retire at a very young age, if she wanted to do so. About four years ago, in reviewing the business, she was losing money for the third straight year.

The reason for the business downturn included competing internet sales, the cost of parking in downtown Minneapolis, increased Lasik eye surgeries, insurance reimbursement cutbacks, increased competition from low-cost operators like Wal-Mart, and higher operating costs.

We recommended Jodie sell the business to one of her long-time employees over a six-year buy-out. Because of her young age, Jodie was able to work for other stores, earn money and increase her income by almost $60,000 per year, versus running the store.

It is easy to just let inertia carry you through life. In Jodie's case, she was depressed about her business in spite of the many good years she had with it. By selling the business, she became free and happy once again.

Is your business costing you money year after year? If so, it is not an investment. In fact, it may make sense to sell it or shut it down. Also, if you profit more from selling your company than working every day you are better off selling it and doing something better with your time.

If your business pays you a salary after all costs, and pays you a reasonable return on your business equity, continue to operate the business. In this case, it is an investment.

Despite your passion for your business, are you working for free or even losing money? Are you going to let momentum or a dream of being a business owner carry you to a poor outcome? Consider instead selling or shutting down operations as your business is or becomes a non-producing asset. Also, consider selling your business if you are paid more by selling it than it will generate for you in the future.

Retirement Accounts – Investments

Retirement accounts are investments. Most annuities, 401(k)s, traditional and ROTH IRAs, 403(b)s, and profit sharing accounts are all investments because you can turn them into a cash flow. Obviously, each account has to be analyzed for performance, but we include all retirement accounts as part of your investments.

There are a few exceptions to exclude. If you have a monthly pension or a fixed payout annuity that cannot be changed, it is not an asset. It is simply income that is reflected in your net income. Fixed payments like a pension or social security payments are neither non-performing assets nor an investment, for the purposes of this book.

Our reasoning has to do with the purpose of identifying non-performing assets versus investments. Identification helps determine how much investments you have now and how much income you will need in order to live off your investment portfolio in the future.

Since these income payments are already income to you, putting them in the investment category would double count their income stream. Therefore, do not include pensions of unchanging fixed payout annuities, but all other liquid stocks, bonds, mutual funds, brokerage accounts or retirement funds would be investments.

Life Insurance – Can Be Either A Non-Producing Asset or an Investment

Life insurance can be an investment or not, depending on its structure. How much of your premium is purely expense, and what is the return on the policy's cash value? To find out the answers to these questions, we separate the cost of insurance and compare the return on the investment portion of the policy to see how the investment portion is doing. In some cases, the after-tax returns are quite satisfactory; in other cases, the returns are not very good.

Life expectancies have increased and the cost of insurance has come down, so review each policy's cost based upon your needs, the policy's replacement value and the policy's investment returns or cash value. We include all cash values as an investment and any net cash outflow as an expense.

Non-Retirement Financial Accounts – Investments

We include mutual funds, direct investments, stocks, private placements, brokerage accounts, bank accounts, and most cash value life insurance as investments, as long as they meet these criteria:

1. You are (or can) receive payments from the investment
2. You do not have to pay in to support it
3. You can sell it, change it, manage it or keep it at your discretion

As long as your non-retirement financial accounts meet these criteria, they are an investment.

Collectables – Can Be Either A Non-Producing Asset or an Investment

Is your collection of baseball cards, farm implements, jewelry, art, cars or land an investment? If you are selling it and it will pay you money, this may be an investment.

Brett collects old books and world art. For example, he recently purchased an English King James version of the Bible published in 1683, just a few years after its original translation into English under the guidance of King James. Over the years he has sold very few books from his antique collection. He has probably lost a few by lending them away and not getting them back! Even though the books and art may appreciate, they would not be an investment based upon how we define it in this book. Unless you plan to sell the collectibles for profit or run it as a business it is not an investment.

How can you turn your collection into an investment? We have clients that collect, buy and sell cars, dolls, art, heavy equipment and horses. Some of them make good money – it is a business for them. For them, collecting is an investment because they use the collectibles to generate revenue. We have other clients who actively buy and sell on eBay, but on average, their hobby consumes cash. In their case the collectibles are non-producing assets.

"Gambling" – Usually Is a Non-Producing Asset

There are "investments" where the odds are against making money, like gambling. For example: commodities, pull-tabs, gold coins, lottery tickets, options, day-trading and buying stocks that sell for less than $5.00 per share are forms of gambling. The odds are stacked against making money in each of these vehicles. We call this gambling. If the odds are against you in making money, then it is not an investment.

In summary, an investment pays you money and a non-producing asset cost you money.

Now, take what you have learned and apply it to your own situation.

Add up your assets and divide them into the two groups: Investments and Non-Producing Assets. Take an inventory of what you have that qualifies and what does not. If you have non-producing assets that do not meet the test, consider changing them so they do qualify, or sell them and use the proceeds to buy investments or to pay off debt. If they do not add or pay, sell them, donate them, or rent them.

> **Action Item:** Write down why you have each asset. Non-producing assets improve your quality of life and investments can pay you money. If you plan on changing a non-producing asset so it can better serve you, write your plan to sell it, by when, and what you'll do with the proceeds to better your situation.

Key Concept #2 - Learn to buy at a bargain, sell when everyone wants "in"

Brady and Joe are brothers with a lot in common. Both are married. Both are from Chicago. Both have three children. Both have good jobs that net them $100,000. So, how are they different? Brady saves $50,000 per year and Joe spends $50,000 more than he makes. This has been happening for more than 10 years. Brady has a great portfolio that pays him money and Joe is in debt up to his eyeballs paying interest, just to support his lifestyle. What little Joe has saved is invested into his checking at less than one percent return. Brady has done well and has made 10.46 percent on his diversified portfolio. Past performance is no guarantee of future results.

Joe had to file bankruptcy after just eight years, and is trying to emerge from the ashes. Brady had saved over $800,000 in a decade, savings that pay him $64,000 per year. Both brothers are very similar, but they see very different financial results.

Here is the secret about great investments. Businesses are no different than you, Brady, or Joe. If a company does not make money, then it is probably not a good investment. Consider investments that make a consistent and satisfactory net income.

Consider Investments that have the Potential to Make Money

In business, savings is compared to net margin or cash flow. Many companies lose money year after year, and investors are surprised when the stock doesn't perform. This is no different from the brother, Joe, who spent more than he made while expecting to someday live off his savings. His prospects for financial success are as remote as those of an investor who buys a stock in a company which cannot make a buck as measured by net income, positive cash flow, income growth rates or profit margin.

If an investor can invest in federally insured CDs or other low-risk investments and make, say 5 percent, why would anybody invest in a company that cannot earn 5 percent? These investors are taking more risk for less return. In asking many investors, we found several reasons investors buy low-profit or no-profit companies: investors like the company products, they may like the company story, they may be caught up in the stock's momentum, or they feel the stock is a bargain, even though the company still loses money every year.

Sometimes investors may simply feel the stock has growth potential in spite of no earnings history at all. Maybe the investors are right, but throwing money at this type of stock is not an investment, it is a gamble.

Loaning money to Joe because he says he will change his spending ways would be a similar gamble – and a bad one at that.

These are all important considerations, but the best indicator that a company will have high margins and growth tomorrow is if it has had high profit margins and growth in the past to the present. It is unlikely Brady will suddenly sink into a negative cash flow lifestyle. We prefer to

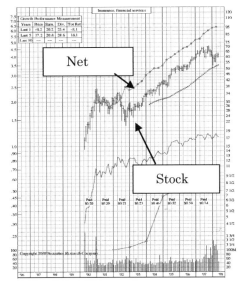

This graph shows net income increasing and stock price following it up.
www.srccharts.com Source: Securities Research Company

look at stock earning histories for 12 years, not 12 months. Short-term company earnings can be manipulated on how revenue and expenses are reported. It is not difficult to shift costs for one year. In viewing company trends for more than a decade however, it is easy to see their tendencies – making and saving money like Brady, or spending more than they make, like Joe.

What about the company's future? We also look at estimates for future cash flow and future earnings growth rates to make sure the income potential hasn't changed going forward. The above chart shows stock net income and stock price over an eight-year period. Pay particular attention to the correlation of company earnings to stock price. Remember, however, past performance is no guarantee of future results.

Return on Assets

Some companies require an extraordinary amount of capital to generate a single dollar of revenue. Some do not. There are companies with a return on assets or return on equity of 50 percent, and there are companies with return on assets of less than one percent. Companies that have simple businesses and a high return on assets are sought after by guru value-based investors like Warren Buffett because companies with higher returns on assets have a greater success rate.

Can you make money investing in companies which lose money and have a low or no return on investment? Of course you can. When Brett wrote The Corporate Guide to Profit & Wealth, he was surprised at the range of experience and industries of those interested in using its lessons. Many organizations wanted and followed our recommendations. But, just like working with individuals, some did not want help and felt like earning profit was not necessary. Instead, they wanted validation – even if they needed to make some changes.

From an Arch Bishop of the Catholic Church, to 100-year-old publicly traded companies, to dot-com companies – many organizations came to us and wanted to know how to improve their bottom lines. The results varied depending on the degree to which a company was willing to change its behaviors.

One Boston-based technology company had us look at their operations. After a brief review, we met with the three founders and told them they needed to make more money – in other words, *increase their cash flow and net profit. The company retorted, "You just do not understand our business. We operate off a 'buy-sales model,' where we spend $1.05 to make a $1.00. Then, we make up the difference in stock price." When we explained that this was an unsustainable long-term business model, they asked us to leave. Within a year their stock dropped 90 percent.*

In Panama City, Fla., in an ocean-front condo building, the average rental property generated a loss for most owners. They lost money after earning rent less the costs of association dues, property taxes, insurance and other owner expenses. Many owners and prospective clients said they could make up the loss in appreciation. Unfortunately, this was a hard and very expensive lesson for many investors when the Florida real estate market tumbled.

Today, so many investors are in default that association dues are going up to the remaining payers—making a bad situation worse. These investors are learning the hard way why they should not include appreciation in their decision on investment property.

Think about the many investments you or people you know have made over the years that are not investments according to our definition. How well did they do? By following some simple rules, many people would have avoided the oil and gas deals of the early 1980s, the real estate correction resulting from the tax law changes in 1986, the junk-bond losses of the early 1990s, the dot-com meltdown of the 2000s, not to mention the market crisis of 2008.

Investing in companies that appear to be money making companies will not help in all cases. For example, if you invested in companies like New Century, WorldCom, MCI and Enron where there was graft, criminality and malfeasance these or any other fundamental investment strategies do not help. Past performance is not a guarantee of future results.

Some of the most valuable insights into a company are their financial statements. If the statements are wrong, even the best analysis of that company will be wrong.

We protect our clients by investing in many different companies. The good news is this: in almost every company, there is a person or group who cares a great deal more about the accuracy of these financial statements than you because of the amount of money they have in it. It could be a founder, a mutual fund or a very large investor.

Look at your investments and ask yourself, "Am I invested in companies or investments that make enough money for the investment risk I take?" Do they pay those gains to the shareholders? Check the validity of the income by looking at net income, profit and cash flow as they relate to share price over many years.

Action Item: List your investments. Do they pass the tests of being great investments? (1) Do they make money? (2) Do they have great cash flow? (3) Do they have the potential to make a great return? If not, sell and replace with investments that do pass.

Key Concept #3 - Make Money After Taxes And Inflation

Jeanne was paid $2 million for the sale of her Minneapolis-based hair products company. And after losing big in the tech bubble, she decided to put all her money into CDs. She figured she could live off the returns of her 6 percent CD, or $120,000 per year. Past performance is no guarantee of future results but, what was her income tax?

According to her accountant, her income tax was 25 percent, or $30,000. And, of course, there was inflation. Gas, medicine, food *and utilities all increased. In fact, inflation has averaged 3.5 percent over the last 20 years, according to the U.S. government, eating up another $70,000 of her income in lost buying power. After taxes and inflation she ended up with a mere $20,000 on her $2 million invested. The bottom line, with $20,000 after taxes and inflation, even $2 million is not enough to cover her $5,000 monthly expenses, if 100% is invested in risk-free investments.*

Example of Jeanne's income, after taxes and inflation on $2 million dollars:

2008 Investment assets invested in bank CDs:	*$2,000,000*
Interest at 6%	*$ 120,000*
Assumed Year End Principle and Interest	*$2,120,000*
Less 25% ordinary income taxes	*($ 30,000)*
Less 3.5% inflation on the $2 million	*($ 70,000)*
Money after taxes and inflation in 2008 dollars:	*$2,020,000*

This only leaves $20,000 of spending money this year or you begin to eat away at the purchasing power of your investments! Just by increasing the return to 10 percent, your return will increase the real rate of return by 300 percent in this example.

This easily illustrates why you need to invest at least a portion of your investments in securities that have returns greater than taxes and inflation even if it means greater risk and volatility. Which investments do you have that do this? Consider keeping some investments in CDs, bonds, annuities, stocks, mutual funds, REITS and real estate.

Action Item: Write in your journal on how your investments do after inflation and taxes. Historically, risk-free investments make very little after taxes and inflation, while stocks and real estate have out-performed taxes & inflation. Write down what best fits your needs.

Bonds / CDS / Annuities

In the previous example we said these didn't pay much, although we do use these for very specific portfolio needs. To get better diversification, we use ETFs or funds instead of specific bond for most investors. We use fixed income investments for risk adverse investors and for their added stability versus other investments, like stocks and real estate. We use bonds to pay taxes or for safe money (if held till maturity) needed for a specific time frame. We use money markets for a rainy day fund.

In Wealth in a Decade, we suggested using a laddered bond portfolio. We still recommend using this strategy for a declining interest rate environment. However, in a low-interest environment with a greater chance of rising interest rates we use variable annuities instead, especially for long-term investing purposes. Why? As interest rates go up, the value of bonds decline. A 10-year bond will lose about 10 percent for every one percent increase in interest rates, not counting the interest the bond pays. Guarantees are based on the claims-paying ability of the issuing insurance company. Bonds can suffer from credit risk, interest-rate risk, default risk, and pricing fluctuations.

Treasury bonds can lose in market value in a rising interest rate environment. Some annuities allow investors to stay invested in higher returning investments, while guaranteeing either the value or the future income percentage. There may be fees and expenses associated with guarantees and riders.

Other considerations for bonds are their ratings, tax handling, duration and liquidity. Since bonds typically represent 'safe' money, we suggest you stick to high-quality bonds while avoiding junk or high-yield specific bonds. Understand how the bond gets its rating, for if it is from bond insurance, any adverse impact on the insuring entity might prove very negative to the value of the bond. Lastly, if it is a corporate bond, buy only those that have great prospects for the company stock.

Stocks

In our business, we look to invest in the stocks of out of favor companies with excellent earning histories and good future earnings growth. Taxes are low if you hold stock for more than 12 months and some pay dividends as well. If you hold them until you die, then your heirs pay no tax on the gains (under current tax law). A portion of your investments should be in higher dividend stocks. High dividend stocks are issued by companies like Kraft Foods (KFT), Pfizer (PFE), or 3M (MMM). We are not endorsing these stocks in particular as good investments; they are used for example purposes only.

Tom Cameron, father of the rising-dividend concept, suggests investing in companies with a good history of increasing dividends. Dividends are taxed at lower rates than ordinary investments, based on current tax laws. Growth stocks are publicly-traded companies that pay investors by growing the value of the stock. Limit your holding to stocks on the NASDAQ, NYSE or AMEQ, and to stocks selling for more than $5.00 per share. These stocks can be converted into cash in three business days. The disadvantage (and advantage) to growth stocks is that the value can vary greatly from day-to-day.

Mutual Funds

Consider investing in mutual funds. These provide professional management and diversification at very low investment amounts.

There are, however, clear disadvantages to mutual funds. These disadvantages are covered in the next chapter.

Real Estate

Every investment must pass the same tests – good profit margins, good return on assets and high relative values. In our analysis of investments for clients, we do not build appreciation into a decision on whether to buy or not. The criteria we use to buy is strict: we only buy if it shows a 10 percent or more return and if it can be bought so that if we need to sell we can, without losing much money.

In a normal real estate market, where possible, we buy at a 10 to 20 percent discount to the true market value, as compared to recent sales. In a depressed market, we will buy at much deeper discounts to the current real estate value. We determine "current value" by analyzing sales made within the last 90 days and by looking at the trend to determine an acceptable offer, so we can build in an acceptable margin for error.

After we buy, we will hold the property until the returns drop to 5 percent, either because of increased costs, reduced rents, or an increased market value of the property. This strategy clearly indicates when to buy, what to buy and when to sell.

When we buy, we want at least a 10 percent cash-on-cash return. As an example, one of our clients owned a building just outside the main gate of Eglin Air Force Base. The rent was a triple net lease, which means the tenant was responsible for all costs, including maintenance, taxes and insurance.

The lease was usually 5 to 10 years and was rented by government military companies needing an approved, top-security clearance servicing the base. As of 2005, the building rented for $4,000 net per month and sold for $460,000. Its return exceeded 10 percent and therefore was a good "buy" opportunity. After we buy a property, if the returns drop below 5 percent, we sell.

For example, a condo we purchased in Boca Raton, Fla., was an excellent buy at $140,000 in 1998. It rented for about $40,000 per year and had annual costs of about $12,500 per year. By 2004, its value went up to $260,000 and the rents came down to $20,000, with costs of almost $15,000. Since the return on assets fell below five percent we sold in October 2005. This is a great place to have a seasoned mentor of how to buy and when to sell. Make sure his or her experience is through several market cycles.

REITS (Real Estate Investment Trusts)

Not interested in buying individual properties, but are still interested in real estate's possibilities? Consider publicly traded Real Estate Investment Trusts (REITS). These offer great dividends and some even offer tax benefits. They also offer liquidity.

As with any stock, they can be sold in three business days. REITs, as with all investments, have some limitations. Publicly traded REITs are subject to wide swings in market pricing; non-traded REITs can have limited liquidity. There are also non-traded REITS that offer unique liquidity provisions that might be a better fit, but consider your risk and seek the advice of a professional and read the prospectus carefully before investing.

Also realize that the company does keep the right to suspend liquidity provisions if it is in the company's best interest. Therefore, make sure the company is currently earning profits above the payout amount, otherwise it is cannibalizing the initial investment. Some REITs are leveraged—meaning they borrow money to pay and maintain their properties. This can give investors greater returns, but also increases the risk of loss.

For example, if real estate property values drop ten percent, an associated REIT that is highly leveraged will be impacted more adversely than one that is unleveraged. Leverage magnifies loss on the downside. Conversely, a leveraged REIT has potential for higher returns in prospering economic years. REITS own a portfolio of properties and may specialize in office space, malls, health care facilities or apartment buildings. Because they trade, the reporting is such that you can get a very good idea of how they are doing before investing.

Other Factors to Consider

Invest worldwide. Invest worldwide. Many good companies trade as ADRs or American Depository Receipts on the NYSE. These companies are US dollar-dominated and report using generally accepted accounting principles based on U.S. tax laws. Investing outside the United States involves additional risks, such as currency fluctuations and economic and political factors. Another way to get worldwide investments, while still buying domestic companies, is to buy stock in companies with significant sales overseas.

Watch insider trading. Watch insider trading. There are many reasons why insiders sell, but only one reason why insiders who work for a company buy their company's stock – because they believe it is a good value. We look at insider trading as a final screen – if all insiders that are "in the know" are selling we don't buy. Conversely, if everyone within the company is buying and the stock shows good margins, good ROAs and is trading at a bargain price, we are very interested.

Make sure most of your investments make a positive return after inflation and taxes. Make sure most of your investments make a positive return after inflation and taxes. The exception is money where liquidity is vital and is needed for a specific time or purpose, like paying taxes or a rainy day fund.

How do your investments rate? Are you invested to make a return after taxes and inflation? Write down what changes you will make (if any) to your individual investments. Past performance is no guarantee of future results.

Key Concept #4 - Learn to Comfortably Ride Up and Down Markets as They "Breathe"

Buy at a bargain, sell when everyone wants it. Great investments can be too expensive or they can be really cheap. This is measured in relative value. When they are expensive, they are generally in favor. Consider buying when a particular stock is out of favor, but still has high future income cash flow and return on assets.

This is very hard to do and goes against human nature. Yet, it is how investors like Warren Buffet have made their fortunes. "Buy when there is fear and sell when there is euphoria," has been Buffet's longstanding mantra. Also, we tend to focus on future profitability not just what they are today. Some investors point out that in 2008 and early 2009, Warren Buffet was down 40%. Could Buffet's investment philosophy be outdated? To answer, let me share an old Chinese proverb that rings true to the modern day investor:

"A middle-aged farmer having farmed for several decades was surprised to find a beautiful wild stallion on his property. His neighbors immediately took notice, and envied this serendipitous find that was sure to increase his fortune. They all 'celebrated' in the horse, and told the farmer how lucky he was. The farmer replied, 'Maybe I am, maybe I'm not.' The next day the stallion broke the leg of the farmer's son. The neighbor's lamented the farmer, whose apparent luck had quickly turned into devastation. What an unlucky man he was. The farmer said, 'Maybe I am, maybe I'm not.' One more day passed, and the Chinese military came into town to take away all the male youth for service. The only son left behind was the farmer's son, whose injury made him unfit for military service. Once again, the bereaving neighbors expressed resentment at the farmer, and he was accused of being 'lucky.' The farmer's response did not change: 'maybe I am, maybe I'm not.' "

In his wisdom, the farmer knew the present situation could not be accurately judged from today's perspective. This is true for investing. We've seen a client demand for us to sell a stock after a 25% drop in price, only to miss out on a 2300% gain afterward! Many investors sell out in a down market just before the market pops and regains recent loss. When an investor buys into an investment portfolio he is expecting the investment to go up.

In fact, over the years we have learned that investors have an unlimited risk tolerance, until the investment goes down. When we buy a stock, we buy it for where we see it going, not where it is now. In fact, since we buy out of favor stocks, it is not unusual for a particular stock to go down on its way to doing very well. We could be wrong about a company's future earnings due to unforeseen events, malfeasance, adverse accounting practices, or just poor timing. The good news is you can be wrong and still do well on average.

Wayne Gretzky, the famous hockey player, was once interviewed on his strategy. When asked what made him so great, he said, "Most players will go where the puck is, I go where the puck will be." We share this approach for investments as well.

This up and down movement is what we call "breathing," and investors must be willing to handle the downs to make the ups. It is not unusual for a stock portfolio to drop as much as 20 to 30 percent in a market contraction. Individual stocks can fluctuate

Action Item: Did you buy your investments at a bargain? Does everyone love or hate them right now? What has been sold off lately that may be a good bargain?

50 percent or more during a year and still be a great long-term investment. To determine a bargain stock, we look at stocks that trade at much higher relative values. Then, we look at future income. In many cases a stock's future relative value is very good in spite of its current unpopularity. Ideally, we buy a beaten down stock that will probably take the market 12 to 24 months to like it again. We are long-term investors, so the short term drop in price has little effect in our considerations.

For example, when insurance companies ran into trouble in 2001 for trading issues, the whole sector was reduced by as much as 50 percent. ING Group (ING) went from a high of $42 down to a low of $10. Met Life (MET) dropped from $34 to $20. AEGON (AEG) dropped from $42 to $6. Past performance is no guarantee of future results. The drops that happened in 2008 were even more dramatic.

Because so many people invested in mutual funds, whole indexes like the S&P 500 and the Dow Jones Industrial Average dropped 50% or more from their peaks. This was a wholesale selloff by institutional investors, and most every stock was affected—even companies with great earning potential! In all three cases, earnings expanded considerably. From 2002 to 2007 their earnings and dividends increased. We are not endorsing these stocks in particular as good investments; they are used for example purposes only.

Have you lost money in investments? Stocks? Bonds? Real Estate? You are not alone. Most investors have lost money.

Losing money in investments can teach you the wrong lessons, just like hitting it big at the casino can teach you "gambling" is the way to riches. We are not fans of using anecdotal evidence as fact, but our 30-plus years of investing experience proves this.

Paul came to us for help in investing $1 million that he and his wife earned in a real estate deal. As we reviewed their holdings, we agreed that since they still had considerable real estate holdings, we would put half the proceeds in fixed income and the other half in stocks. They were already debt free.

We started buying 50 percent of the assets intended for stocks with the idea that we would dollar cost average the rest over the next six months. After one month, we got a call from Paul asking why the account was down 1/10 of 1 percent. Before buying, we discussed the fact that stocks do go up and down, and Brett and Josh asked how they would feel if their investments dropped. Paul's answer was he was "looking at long-term growth." And yet, this small movement worried him greatly. Brett suggested he decide – either let your account "breathe" or do not invest in stocks. After three months, his account was still below its original investment.

Paul was getting impatient, so we decided it would be better to have someone else manage his money. After three months and being only partially invested, Paul could not handle market ups and downs. Within 90 days the market rebounded, hitting an all-time high, and our accounts responded with equal gains. As our accounts climbed up, Brett was sad knowing that Paul had chosen to be left behind.

Before you invest, you'll need to ask yourself if you can handle the downturns and the risks that go along with the returns. If you can't bear to watch the market breathe—and it will as it always has—you may want to consider whether you truly should be in the market. Deciding not to invest is better than lying in bed at 3:00am worrying about your stocks. In that case keep investments limited to ones that are guaranteed.

Over time diversified portfolios have done well. There are times where markets are down and the successful long-term investor has to be able to ride out the pullbacks. In addition not all investments will make money. Some will be poor investments. For example, consider setting investment standards for yourself. You have to be willing to withstand a little unrealized loss to make real profit in the future. Part of my goal with this book is to help you refine your criteria of "good" and "bad" investments so that you, like many people, do not avoid an entire sector, just because profit, cash flow and returns were not completely understood.

For example:

• Stocks: Consider buying profitable companies with good future prospects trading at $5.00 or more.

• Real Estate: Consider buying properties that earn 10 percent or more after all costs. If your returns drop because of increased costs, decreased rents or appreciated value, consider selling.

• Bonds/CDs/Money Markets: Do you have regular amounts of money coming due to take advantage of market movement? Do you have enough in your rainy day fund to help in emergencies, to pay taxes or help with your kids' college?

Learn to comfortably ride the ups and downs of the markets as they "breathe."

I believe strongly that money is a multiplier. If you put good things through it, good things will happen. Now that you know how to invest, the next chapter will help you with your asset allocation – which will greatly impact your investment success.

Key Concept #5: Active Investing (Buy and Hold No Longer Works)

For decades, many investors have employed what is called a "buy and hold" investment strategy. Instead of actively managing your portfolio by rebalancing—buying and selling positions—typical investing tells you to purchase investments with the intention of holding them indefinitely, no matter the change in market conditions. This is a particularly attractive strategy for many investors because it does not require the time commitment or active research required to maintain a flexible portfolio.

In contrast to this, and confirmed by what we have seen in the markets in the early twenty-first century, investors must take an active role in their investing by both shedding unpromising holdings and buying new and promising opportunities. The "buy and hold" investor did very well holding stock in General Electric and Ford Motor Company (long-time trusted companies) through the 1980's and 1990's. However, that same investor would have lost most of their gains, if not all, by continuing to hold those stocks through today. This example is for illustration purposes, and not a recommendation.

The "buy and hold" strategies of earlier decades worked well in a stock market that saw consistent growth with relatively little turbulence. Your investment portfolio today requires much more active rebalancing. For most investors, professional assistance is a great asset to improve the diligence of your investing strategy.

Key Concept #6: The Key Factor to Making Money in Any Investment – The Selling Discipline

Remember, you do not make money when you buy something. You make money when you sell it, and only if you do so at a profit. Our goal is to make sure that we put our clients' money in at the lowest risk possible, thereby stacking the odds in their favor. There are no guarantees. Let the profits run as long as possible, but most importantly, have a predetermined methodology to take that money out and put it in your account.

The most important investment practices are the procedures that guide you in entering and exiting the market. We have all heard stories of sweet stocks turned sour. How many times have you heard someone's story about how invincible a certain stock was, only to watch it drop after you add it to your own portfolio? Go back to the tech boom of the late nineties and into 2000. Millions of people would love to be able to go back and pull out of the market in late 1999 or in early in 2008, but didn't, because their greed got in the way.

The market preys upon emotional investors. By having a mechanical process, you remove yourself from your instinctive emotions. Remember: your head is on top of your heart for a reason: it's supposed to control it. Having systematic procedures keeps that relationship in sync.

Every investor is different, and no one investing model effectively works in all markets. Most will lose money at some point. Most everyone would agree to be "risk averse"—we do not like to risk losing our money needlessly. There are, however, varying degrees of risk tolerance among investors. If you are an aggressive investor, you are willing to see large potential gains for the chance of also enduring slumps in your portfolio values. If, on the other hand, you like safety, surety, and consistency in your investments, you should invest in a similar manner with realistic expectations on your potential gains and losses.

Market signals can help assist you in identifying riskier and less risky periods. Typically, we see a change in the market trends two to three times a year, but this can vary. Our research is based off of both fundamental and technical analysis. Your investing pattern should be broadly diversified over a number of different asset classes including: direct investments, annuities, domestic stocks, international stocks, domestic bonds, international bonds, commodities, and currencies. By being proactive you will be able to grow your wealth and preserve what you already have.

Human nature works against successful investing. Our emotions drive us to put money into what has done well and take away from what has done poorly. The successful investor has learned to sell when everyone is enamored and buy when others are fearful.

SUMMARY

1. Understand what makes an asset an investment which makes money, or a non-performing asset which costs money. If your non-performing assets do not meet their

intended purpose, sell them and use the proceeds to reduce debt or to increase your investments that make money.

2. Learn what makes an investment a great investment. Specifically, it needs to have the potential to make money, provide adequate cash flow and be purchased at a good price.

3. Invest where the odds are in your favor after taxes and inflation. Do not gamble. Make sure you have stocks and real estate in your investment portfolio. Use cash and bonds for specific needs – a rainy day fund, tax bill or safe money.

4. Learn to buy at a bargain and sell when everyone wants in.

5. Invest knowing market pricing will go up and own. Know the markets will "breathe." The lack of expectation of a down market is why investors have not done well in their investments. Understanding why investments do well should make investing seem less arbitrary and increase your odds of not selling out at the bottom and doing well in the long run. Make sure you are following each key item in your asset structure and in your buy/sell decisions. Use the guidelines for each type of investment to get the most "buy" for your investment buck. If this is too overwhelming to do on your own, please ask a professional for help.

6. Successful investing in the twenty first century will require far more active management than in past decades. For most investors, professional assistance is a great help to improve the diligence of your investing strategy.

> *Human nature works against successful investing. Our emotions drive us to put money into what has done well and take away from what has done poorly. The successful investor has learned to sell when everyone is enamored and buy when others are fearful.*

IV. THE ESSENTIALS TO EFFECTIVE DIVERSIFICATION

Disclosure: *The investments discussed may not be suitable for all investors. Investors must make their own decisions based on their specific investment objectives, risk tolerances and financial circumstances. An individual's results may vary from the client situations stated in this chapter. The information presented is meant as an illustration only. It is not indicative of any specific return or yield on a particular investment.*

*J*ohnny could have been a poster child for **Wealth in a Decade**, my previous book, which covered how to achieve wealth in a reasonable amount of time. He and his wife lived modestly on his $50,000 per year government retirement pension. What's more – they were completely debt-free, as they owned their home free and clear since they purchased it 25 years ago. However, when a bank CD came due, Johnny's local bank loan officer suggested they get a mortgage, to increase their tax deductions and increase their income.

In 25 years his quiet bayside home appreciated 8 fold. They took a $1 million dollar home equity line of credit on their $1.25 million dollar home in December 2006, and followed the advice of their bank to put the entire proceeds into mortgage subprime debentures recommended by the young bank investment representative.

"These pay almost 1.5 percent more than the 6.6 percent mortgage rate you're charged, which should increase your income by $15,000, while creating a large tax deduction!" according to the advisor.

The plan looked great on paper. However, by the end of 2007, their $1 million dollar investment portfolio was worth $379,000. They had lost 62 percent of their investment portfolio, and are still *saddled with a $1 million mortgage and the $66,000 in annual payments that go along with it.*

How did he turn it around?

Johnny has gone back to work and is digging himself out of the debt as quickly as he can. He is also trying to sell their home to cut down their expenses. The good news is that he has high-income potential and will be able to recover from the loss in about five years of full-time work based upon his savings and return assumptions.

Most people pay heavily for financial mistakes relating to the lack of diversification, one of the more common and understandable mistakes we see. Unfortunately, most learn the wrong lesson. In most cases, they begin to believe that all investing is bad rather than revise how to properly invest. For example, a person might have lost money because they invested in tech stocks that did not make money. In the long-term, this just hurts them by either having a non-diversified portfolio that has no stocks or it creates over-concentration in other asset classes. In many cases there is a specific reason why they lost money. Simply investing in money-making and cash-flowing stocks that are purchased out of favor will increase your money-making possibilities versus buying stocks that consume cash.

Here are a few more examples:

Paul, a long-time client recently sold his company. He was debt-free and had a diversified portfolio of stocks, bonds and real estate. As Florida real estate began its boom, Paul slowly increased his real estate holdings. Before too long, Paul had 80 percent of his wealth in Florida real estate just before its peak in 2005. Paul went from having no debt to being highly leveraged. He went from a safe, conservative investment position to a risky and speculative one. In the end he lost it all.

Mabel, the mom of a long-time client, was 100-percent invested in junk bonds in 1990. Her money was managed by a local bank. We suggested she diversify. Luckily, months before the junk bond crash, she listened and her nest egg was preserved.

Bart was a modest investor and great saver. He invested primarily in mutual funds, but because the best performing funds were invested in tech stocks in 1999, he moved all his mutual funds into tech stocks. By the end of 2001, Bart had lost 60 percent of his funds and decided never to invest in stocks again. Bart never recognized that his losses were due to investing in companies which couldn't make money. Instead, he learned the wrong lesson—that all stocks are bad.

These stories highlight the importance of diversification.

WHAT IS DIVERSIFICATION?

Diversification is simply not putting all of your eggs into one basket. It is investing in such a way as to minimize your exposure from any one event devastating your nest egg. Diversification, however, does not ensure a profit or protect against loss in a declining market. The acid test of proper diversification is if the investment portfolio components move up or down at the same time. If all the components do, you are not diversified.

As mentioned in earlier chapters, consider investing in money market funds, bank CDs, bonds, income stocks, growth stocks, mutual funds, real estate and annuities. These investments can be tied to companies in the United States, global companies, or government-issued securities.

Wealth in a Decade covered how to buy low and sell high, or more accurately, how to sell high, and then put the proceeds into the asset classes that are down. How do you do this? You buy investments in completely different asset classes while still following the successful investing concept outlined in the prior chapter, specifically – fixed income, equities and real estate.

A year later, you'll see that each asset class responded to the economy differently. For example one might have gone up, one might have stayed the same and one might have gone down.

By simply comparing each investment to its value when you bought it a year earlier, you'll know if it went up or down without guessing. Then, sell enough when the values are high and add to the asset classes trading lower. We call this rebalancing your portfolio.

The ongoing goal is to have the same amount invested in each asset class. Here is a practical example. You buy three investment classes:

$100,000 in Fixed-Income investments
$100,000 in Stocks
$100,000 in Real Estate
$300,000 Total investments

In one year, which class will have performed the best? The funny and true answer is we do not know for sure and neither does anyone else. Imagine that a year later they were worth this:

$110,000 in Fixed-Income Investments -- up 10%
$125,000 in Stocks -- up 25%
$ 95,000 in Real Estate -- down 5%
$330,000 Total Investments went up 10%

Which investments are high? Obviously the stocks, which were up 25 percent. Which investments were lowest? Obviously, the real estate, which was down 5 percent. According to our strategy, we sell $15,000 of stocks at a high and buy $15,000 of real estate which is at a low.

Here is the same investment portfolio a year and a day later after we sold high and then bought low to bring each asset class to equal holdings within the portfolio:

$110,000 in Fixed-Income investments
$110,000 in Stocks
$110,000 in Real estate
$330,000 Total investments

Each year you follow the same steps to re-balance. This simple strategy should add to your returns over time. But it is not what most investors do. Most people get "mad" at the investment class that went down and "punish" it by selling it when it is low. In fact, we have lost clients because the stock market went down 20 percent and their overall portfolio went down 2 percent. Instead of adding to stocks at a low, they moved them into investments that were already at a high. This is a big, but common mistake. They reward the investment that went up and added to it. The result is investors become over-concentrated at the very worst time - at a high.

It is important to pick asset classes in your basket of investments that have a history of not trading together. For example, if everything is up or if everything is down at the same time, moving from one investment to another does not help lower your costs or help you financially. If you have different non-correlated assets, moving them can lower the overall investment costs, portfolio volatility and helps capitalize in the market "breathing."

Are you in an over-concentrated position or are you diversified? Here is a look at several non-correlated assets – fixed income, stocks and real estate – and what they can do for you.

ASSET SELECTION – How Do Broad Investment Categories Work

Fixed Income or Cash Equivalents

Cash Equivalents

Checking accounts, savings accounts and money market accounts are very important in a diversified portfolio. These investments pay interest with very little risk. Their main advantage is that they can be converted to cash on demand. Their disadvantages are that they pay the lowest return and are taxed at the highest income tax rate – ordinary income.

Fixed-Income Investments

Bank CDs, low-risk, short-duration, highly rated bonds and other low-risk fixed income investments offer higher returns than savings or money markets in exchange for less access to your money.

Their advantage is a high degree of safety. Their disadvantage is that they pay investors lower returns than riskier investments and are less liquid than money market funds. Also, rating changes can severely affect a bond portfolio. We saw this happen in the middle of the 2008 crisis when the bond insurers were downgraded by rating services. Bonds are usually taxed at the highest income tax rate–ordinary income. Fixed investments that offer tax advantages pay less, usually by the difference of the tax savings over similar taxable investments. For example municipal bonds usually pay even less as compared to taxable bonds.

Consider each of the risks that impact fixed income investments like:
- Duration
- Default
- Withdrawal penalties
- Creditworthiness
- Currency risk for international bonds

There is more duration risk on longer bonds and less on shorter bonds. Default risk has to do with the credit quality of the issuer. The poorer the credit the more likely the bonds will default; higher risk bonds pay a higher interest rate, but your risk of losing it all is greater. Withdrawal penalties have to do with the penalties imposed if you need your money sooner than when the investment comes due. Creditworthiness has to do with the interim value loss if the issuer or bond insurer over-extends themselves, like what happened to AMBAC municipal bond insurance early in 2008. The insured bond dropped in market value because of problems with the insuring company. Currency risk has to do with the value fluctuations of foreign currencies relative to the US dollar.

When selecting an investment ask your advisor how each risk impacts the suggested investment.

Bob is a conservative investor and retired banker from Texas. He just turned 69 and has his priorities straight. He loves his wife, Judy and takes very good care of himself physically. He is as smart as they come, and has learned many life lessons over the years. Every time we meet, we talk for hours.

Bob spends a great deal of his time helping others, including myself, as he shares many lessons learned in his 50 years of banking.

Bob is risk adverse and makes sure he can live solely off his CD interest. He then supplements his investment income with our investment portfolios and his own real estate "deals" as they pop up. His fixed income investments provide him with a fantastic lifestyle, without having to worry about the ups and downs of the market.

Annuities

Annuities can be a good way to add safety to your portfolio. There are many different types of annuities from which to choose, and unfortunately, they can be complex. The advantages differ depending on the types of annuities. Annuities are usually difficult to fully understand, which can be the main disadvantage for using them. There are three basic types of annuities, fixed, indexed and variable..

Fixed Annuities generally pay a fixed rate over a specific time, much like a CD, except they are not FDIC insured. When you consider these investments, make sure the guaranteed interest rate is for the same period as the withdrawal penalties. Some contracts offer very high "trust me rates" for short periods, much like a zero interest credit card. You start out at zero; however, the credit card quickly converts to high-interest rates and high fees. Guarantees are based on the claims-paying ability of the issuing insurance company. The same can be true of fixed-rate annuities that pay very high rates, some as high as ten percent for a few months. But, because you are locked in for a longer period, when the high rate is done, you are stuck in the worst of two choices – earning low returns, or paying stiff early withdrawal penalties. Also, consider contracts that offer penalty-free withdrawals in less than seven years. Lastly, be wary of bonus rates, as they can end up paying less over the contract, because of additional fees and expenses associated with bonus rates.

Equity-indexed annuities (EIAs) are complex financial instruments that have characteristics of both fixed and variable annuities. Their return varies more than a fixed annuity, but not as much as a variable annuity. EIAs give you more risk (but more potential return) than a fixed annuity but less risk (and less potential return) than a variable annuity. EIAs offer a minimum guaranteed interest rate combined with an interest rate linked to a market index. Because of the guaranteed interest rate, EIAs have less market risk than variable annuities. EIAs also have the potential to earn returns better than traditional fixed annuities when the stock market is risky.

If you are considering an equity-index annuity, ask the following questions:

(a) "Can I get an illustration showing how the contract did over five, 10 and 15 years?" Look to see how the contract did over different market periods and decide if the contract makes sense for you.

(b) "When can I withdraw my money and what are the penalties?" Here, you are looking for a date and time you can access your money, without annuitizing the contract or paying a penalty. If it has no liquidity, consider other investments.

(c) *"Once I annuitize the money, what interest will I be paid on my money above return of principle"?* Some contracts pay as little as one-half of one percent once you begin the distribution phase of the annuity contract. If they will not tell you a specific return, consider other options.

Julie is a lucky lady. According to her doctor, she should already be dead. Over the last decade Julie has suffered one illness after another. But not all was bad for Julie. A long-time friend passed away unexpectedly. This friend knew Julie stressed over money, so she left Julie $100,000 in her will. After attending several investment seminars, Julie decided to put her newfound wealth into an indexed annuity.

She just made the decision to invest all her money into one particular equity-indexed annuity that promised to pay 60 percent of the market gains and never lose money.

Another good friend of Julie's suggested she talk to us first. She learned the importance of liquidity. The recommended annuity offered none – that's right – no liquidity at all! If Julie needed money for an emergency or to upgrade her car, she could not get anything but the monthly annuitized payments.

Also, the higher returns based on market participation were only paid during the contract's 'accumulation' phase. Her plans were to immediately receive income, so the high returns discussed in the 'accumulation' phase turned out to be less than one-half of one percent in the 'distribution phase.' After we pointed that out, she opted for diversifying her new-found wealth in several different investments that offered better liquidity and potentially better returns.

Variable Annuities offer a guaranteed death benefit and many specific annuity contracts offer other guaranteed asset and income options. The advantage of variable annuities is they offer various income and asset guarantees. You can also rebalance your assets without creating a taxable event. Some variable annuities offer an insured stock portfolio or guaranteed minimum income options.

The potential disadvantages are the annuity's internal costs which may include higher fees and expenses for death benefits and riders, and potentially higher tax rates. Variable annuities also tend to be very complex; to understand the differences between the good contracts and bad contracts an investor must read the fine print. It is important to understand your liquidity. Some annuities offer 10 percent, per year that you can access penalty-free. Consider no more than ten-year contracts that offer 100-percent access to your balances, penalty-free at some point in the next ten years.

Find out how much the annual fees are and how the guarantees work. Make sure you do not have to annuitize the contract to access your money. Ensure there are good investment options within the contract, as well as a plan of how you will manage the investment options within the contract to changing market conditions. You should consider the investment objectives, risks, charges and expenses of a variable annuity carefully before investing. This and other information can be found in the prospectus for the contract and its underlying investment options. Please read the prospectus carefully before investing. To obtain a prospectus for a variable annuity, contact your financial advisor or the insurance company directly.

Other important things to look for in annuities are ratings of the insurance company, penalty-free access to both the interest and principle within a reasonable timeframe, annuity costs, and flexible investment options within the contract. Avoid annuity contracts with high withdrawal penalties, high internal fees, long surrender periods and contracts with no liquidity without annuitizing the contract.

Cheryl is very risk adverse. "I do not want to lose what I have." She wanted the bulk of her investments guaranteed. So, before investing we helped her pay off every bill under the sun including her Atlanta, Ga., condo and a brand-new Volvo sedan.

We then invested the remaining assets using mostly fixed-investments, conservative dividend stocks and an insured investment portfolio within a variable annuity. Between her interior design business and her investment returns, Cheryl lives comfortably on a fraction of her income. "I was not sure I could make it on my own."

Cheryl's husband ran the finances while they were married for more than 30 years. But now, six years since their divorce, Cheryl has more money than she started with, and a much greater sense of control and freedom.

Stocks

Dividend Stocks

Our definitions of high dividend stocks are stocks that trade on major exchanges and pay a minimum of 4 percent in dividends. They can be in any industry, from oil to shipping, utilities to commercial real estate, financial stocks or even ADRs invested in other countries. To be in our dividend stock portfolio they need to pay a minimum of 4 percent, and earning enough to afford the dividend. These dividends are usually taxed at the lowest possible income tax rates – dividend rates – which can be as much as 50 percent less than the tax on ordinary income.

Other factors to consider are the same with any investment – consistency and levels of the company's net income, growth, cash flow, bargain price, volatility, outlook and industry. These stocks can be converted into cash in three business days. Usually, the disadvantage (or advantage) of dividend stocks is that the value can vary greatly from day to day.

Dave has used his dividend stock income to live on for more than a decade before he qualified for Social Security benefits. Dave had a motorcycle accident at 52. After working as a Kmart department manager for more than 25 years, they let him go because they contended that the injuries affected his ability to work. After becoming a client, we sensed Dave was becoming defined by his motorcycle accident because of the time it took, the lawyers and the change it caused in his life.

"Move on with your life," Brett said.

At first Dave did not appreciate my frankness. Later he relocated from Pittsburgh to just outside of Albuquerque, N. Mex. To this day, Brett shudders when he thinks of how little Dave and his wife Lois had in their retirement funds, but high portfolio returns and low taxes were essential for them. For this reason, we put a significant portion of his portfolio into high dividend stocks. It was a tremendous pressure to meet their expectations, but last year after a decade of living off his portfolio, Dave began receiving Social Security, thereby reducing his portfolio income requirements sustainability.

Unexpectedly, Brett got a book from Dave, **The Five People You Meet in Heaven**, *by Mitch Albom with a note from Dave, "You're one of my five." As he read it, Brett realized two things. (1) You don't always know the impact you have on others; Dave probably paid Brett the highest compliment of his career. (2) Do not read this book in a public place. The end is a tear jerker. Brett read it while working out on a stair climber at the gym and was crying his eyes out.*

Growth Stocks

Growth stocks are publicly-traded companies that pay investors by growing the value of the stock rather than from dividends. We limit our holding to stocks on the NASDAQ, NYSE or AMEQ and these pay less than 4 percent in dividends. These stocks can usually be converted into cash in three business days and can be bought or sold at small spreads, or the difference between the stock's buy and sell. The disadvantage (and advantage) to growth stocks is the value can vary greatly from day to day.

Taxes are low if held long-term and some pay dividends as well. Our goal is to buy stocks we want to hold onto for a long, long time. If successful, the value of the growth portfolio grows, and you end up with significant unrealized capital gains. Stocks are sold if its earnings prospects are adversely impacted or the stock is trading at euphoric levels. Each year we offset gains and losses in non-retirement accounts to minimize tax. As with dividend stocks, consider the co-factors that make a good long-term stock – consistency and levels of the company's net income, growth, cash flow, bargain price, volatility, outlook and industry. Diversify by industry, country, and how each stock reacts to adverse economic events.

My oldest client Bill, and youngest client, Analisa, had two things in common – each did not need much income from their investment portfolio. Both have been long time clients of mine for more than 20 years now.

Bill, at 93, received more from his 3M pension than he spent. The growth stocks in his diversified portfolio allowed his investments to grow, without EVER paying taxes on their growth. Last year, Bill passed away with significant unrealized gains and the IRS exempts those gains from income tax. Bill earned money for decades on some of his stocks and never had to pay taxes on their growth.

Several years before Bill died, he left his estate to his foundation that benefited Bill's college, community and church. Having outlived most of his family and friends, Bill's biggest fear was being alone. With a group of close friends, we made sure that in the end, Bill was with loved ones every day.

Abby, 3 and Bill, 93

Over the last year of Bill's life, Brett's children - Abby (age 3), Ashley (age 6), Jonathan (15) and Nikki (my wife) visited Bill almost every other day. After his death, Brett's youngest daughter asked Nikki and Brett as they put her to bed, "Where's Bill?" They answered, "He is in heaven cooking dinner with his wife, Gaynold. We're all a sure they are cooking something wonderful together in heaven, as that is what they loved doing while here on earth."

Analisa became a client when her mom was tragically murdered for an insurance settlement. At the time, Analisa was just two years old. From then on, Brett was involved in every significant financial decision that affected her. Seeing this sweet little girl grow into a beautiful woman was a true gift. As her mother's sister raised her, there was little demand from the portfolio, so we invested using primarily growth stocks, and fewer fixed income investments.

When Analisa married we were invited to the wedding. Afterward, she sent us a note, "Thank you for being there all of my life." That simple note made what we do seem so appreciated and personal.

Analisa and "Max"

Thank you, Analisa for the gift of being in your life.

A trusted financial advisor can be much more than just a number cruncher. Take the time to seek out someone who matches your lifestyle and your philosophy. Find a good fit and you'll have a trusted advisor at your side for all of life's ups and downs.

Real Estate

We believe real estate is a very important building block in a non-correlated investment portfolio. This real estate might be a rental property, a commercial building, a REIT or in a private placement. We do not build appreciation into our analysis of real estate as to whether to buy or not. The criteria we use to buy is a 10 percent or more return on investment and buying in such a way so that if we need to sell, we can, without losing money.

In a normal real estate market, we suggest you buy at a discount to the true market value, by looking at recent sales. In a depressed market, we will buy at much cheaper discounts to the current real estate value. We determine "current value" by analyzing comparable actual real estate sales made within the last 90 days and by looking at the trend to determine an acceptable offer.

After we buy, we suggest clients hold the property until the returns drop to no less than 5 percent, either because of increased costs, reduced rents, or an increased market value of the property. This strategy clearly indicates when to buy and when to sell. This strategy has kept our clients out of lots of bad real estate investments. If you do not want to own individual properties, consider real estate investment trusts (REITS).

Dave, a developer in Nashville, Tenn., has been successful in business long before he came to us. When we looked at his business, Dave was spending a great deal in rent for his office building. By using the unique skills of Dave's commercial real estate business, he was able to turn his rent into another income source.

Using his own company to do the work, he bought the property from a distressed seller, fixed it up for a fraction of what it would cost anyone else, and it reduced his overall office costs. Dave made almost 50 percent upon completion of his office based upon the final appraisal, and when he retires he will have triple-net rental income that single-handedly can cover 100% of his personal expenses.

Other Non-Correlated Investments

Direct Investments

There are several investments which do not have stock market risk. These can include non-traded real estate investment trusts (REITS), direct oil and gas limited partnerships, leasing opportunities and Tenants In Common transactions. These investments can offer you a good return, but with a very low correlation to publicly-traded stocks, bonds or other types of real estate. There are several direct investments that offer opportunity. Leasing an apartment, nursing home, office, retail real estate, or investing in oil/gas corporations can all be quality direct investments.

The main advantages to these investments are that they are non-correlated to publicly traded stocks and fixed-income investments. They can potentially pay good distributions; they can potentially offer a broad range of tax advantages; also, they can potentially pay good returns (although past returns do not offer guarantees of future results).

Their main disadvantages are they are complex, offer limited reporting, have net worth and income requirements to be able to buy, and have limited liquidity. These are considered long-term investments and should be undertaken only by those investors who can afford to lose all the money invested. The considerations for evaluating these opportunities are structure, liquidity provisions, reputation, costs and exit strategy.

Leasing

For many corporations, leasing is a better alternative to buying equipment. These leases can be for medical equipment, car fleets, heavy equipment, computers, planes or other office equipment.

Real Estate

There are several types of real estate direct investments: land, subdivisions, apartments, malls and shopping centers, developments, hotels, resort homes or office space.

Robert, who lives in the rural city of Red Wing, Minn., loves the private placement he made almost 20 years ago in an apartment building located in Duluth, Minn. Since his original investment, the quarterly payments increased significantly over the years. Several times the general partners of the private placement refinanced the building and passed on the capital distributions to its limited partners. The annual payments are about 25 percent of his original investment 20 years ago. The refinancing returned his original investment over a decade ago, and has continued to rise over time.

> **Action Item:** Refer to your list of classified investments. Have your assets passed the test of diversification? Are you over-concentrated in any one asset type? Are you diversifying by buying low and selling high?

Oil / Gas / Coal

Because of our country's goal to lessen fuel independence, these direct investments can offer excellent tax advantages. Other oil and gas opportunities include producing wells and known reserves.

We do extensive due diligence before considering any of these investments for clients. The factors we consider most important are the experience of the management team, liquidity provisions, upside and downside risks of the particular investment and suitability to the client.

Let's review how to construct a diversified investment portfolio and how to use different types of accounts to meet your needs. The basic types of accounts are checking, non-qualified brokerage accounts, mutual funds, and retirement accounts.

TYPES OF INVESTMENT ACCOUNTS

Expense Checking Accounts

Cash equivalent funds are used to fund your cash needs and emergency funds. We recommend you have at least three to six months of expenses in savings or money market accounts. Use three months if your income is constant. Use six months if your income varies greatly or your job is at risk.

Setting up controls on spending is very important to financial security. We suggest having a dedicated account just for bills. The goal is to know exactly how much you spend each month. If you own a business, set up the same system for your company. A spending account has no wages, pensions, Social Security, interest, sales bonuses, annuity payments or distributions paid to it – it is just for all of your expenses.

But, include all expenses. Monthly bills, credit card balances paid off monthly, gifts, planned (or unplanned) purchases, debt pay-off and support of children all pass through this expense account. Keep a set amount here – we recommend at least two times your average monthly expenses.

Then, once per year, if you add up the 12 transfers from your investment account, you will know exactly what you spend to the penny. Pay off all bills each month, including credit card bills, via this expense account so debt and balances cannot climb. If you are not depositing at least 10 percent more into the investment account than you transfer call our offices at 952-831-8243 and we will send you a guide to help with 78 ways to improve your cash flow.

Troy spent money, but he had no idea how much. "I'm not a detail person." By setting up the expense account where all his expenses are paid without income going in, he finally knew what he spent. Then once a month he moved enough into his spending account to bring the balance to $20,000.

It is a simple concept, but without getting a handle on his outflow it would not be possible to know if he was saving ten percent or not. By adding up the twelve monthly transfers, Troy knew he spent $108,633 last year for his VISA, monthly bills, taxes, purchases, gifts and travel. He then compared that to his $138,300 in net income to determine his savings.

Income Accounts

Deposit all income here (wages, pensions, Social Security interest, tax refunds, annuity payments and distributions). Whatever you earn, make sure your spending is no more than 90 percent of your income. Then, each month, move enough to the expense account to bring it up to your set balance. The only expense to pay out of this account is any income taxes you owe. For example, if your net after-tax income is $120,000 or $10,000 per month if you are routinely spending more than $9,000 per month as evidenced by the monthly transfers into your expense account, you know you are spending too much. If you have income and bills going in and out of the same account at the same time, it makes it very difficult to know where you stand in term of savings and spending.

Most clients use their non-qualified account as the income account so they earn the most money market interest. Others prefer to have their income account at the same bank as their expense checking account then move savings to their investment account as a second step using outline bank transfers.

Consider using whatever works best for you as long as you know what you make as net income, what you save, and what you spend monthly.

Credit Cards

Keep two credit cards with available credit limited to one month's spending. Use one and keep the second just as a backup. Pay off your credit card every month from your expense account. If married and one spouse has a spending problem, consider a credit card limited to $1,000. If you do not limit card use, as a couple, your spending will not likely be controlled.

Non-Qualified Brokerage Accounts

Have a brokerage account where you move at least 10 percent from your income account every month. This will force some funds into savings every month. Start off using mutual funds, direct investments and annuities. Then, as you have more money to work with, consider individual stocks, which offer significant tax advantages.

Consider using half of your monthly savings to pay more towards your debt, until you are debt-free, as covered in the cash flow chapter.

To illustrate, here is how the three accounts work together:

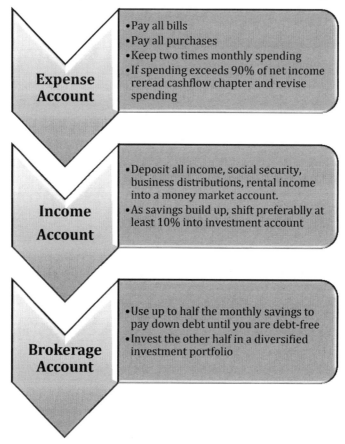

Expense Account
- Pay all bills
- Pay all purchases
- Keep two times monthly spending
- If spending exceeds 90% of net income reread cashflow chapter and revise spending

Income Account
- Deposit all income, social security, business distributions, rental income into a money market account.
- As savings build up, shift preferablly at least 10% into investment account

Brokerage Account
- Use up to half the monthly savings to pay down debt until you are debt-free
- Invest the other half in a diversified investment portfolio

For example, let's say you owe $48,000 in consumer debt and you save $2,000 per month, into your brokerage account. Consider putting $1,000 per month to debt retirement. Once you are consumer debt-free, put any normal consumer debt payments and the $1,000 per month to your mortgage.

Before you know it, you'll be debt free! You will also have a sizable investment portfolio.

> **Action Item:** Have you set up separate income, expense and savings (investment) accounts? Do you pay yourself at least 10% before income can go toward expenses? Do you have a system of tracking income/expenses/savings every month? Consult with your advisor about which accounts are most appropriate for your situation.

Retirement Accounts

401(k)s:

Participate in retirement accounts at your company at least to the extent they match your contributions. For example, if your company matches the first 6 percent at 50 percent, you'll earn 50 percent for every deposit you make up to 6 percent.

If your company does not offer a match, but you spend everything that hits your paycheck, max out the retirement accounts. If you would save anyway, it might be better to reduce the contribution and pay off debt. If you leave the company, put your funds into a retirement account where you have more investment options.

There are usually better options found by moving the assets to a more flexible IRA, rather than leaving them in a 401(k) at a company after you leave.

IRAs:

Consider keeping your IRAs consolidated to allow for simplified recordkeeping and usually, cost savings. As you start out, use mutual funds or exchange traded funds, but as more assets are accumulated, consider individual stocks and annuities.

Many investors add money to an IRA without getting a tax deduction. We believe it is better long-term to develop a non-qualified account, instead of adding to an IRA, particularly if there are no tax advantages beyond tax deferral on the gains. These deferral options still exist in non-retirement accounts with greater access, no penalties and better long-term tax advantages. In making a Roth IRA decision, consider looking at the tax consequences before deciding to convert.

Children's Accounts

Consider funding college monthly out of your expense account. We recommend using an UTMA, UGMA or 529 plans to fund college expenses. Also, have grandparents and your children themselves add to these accounts.

Somehow, children need to move from being completely dependent to being independent, and the job of a good parent is to help in that transition. So, as early as possible, take care of their "needs" and let them earn the extra money to pay for their "wants." Teach them right away to put 20 percent of all gifts and savings into their UTMA/UGMA account. Later, it can pay for college, cars and down payments or a home.

If you don't teach good working and saving skills when your kids are young, both you and they could pay for it the rest of your lives. Require that your children work outside the home no later than age 16. Also, students who work while in college generally do better in school and even after they enter the workforce. Have kids involved in their investments by accompanying you to meet with their advisor at least once per year, as soon as they are age 16.

Mutual Funds vs. Exchange Traded Funds (ETFs)

Throughout this book, we have generally suggested exchange-traded funds (ETFs) over mutual funds. Here is why.

Typical investors and savers generally do not have the time, money or know-how to build their own diversified and strategic portfolios. For these investors, the easy solution to this is buying into a mutual fund. After all, mutual funds are the primary investment vehicle offered in over 90% of retirement plans – including 401(k)s, IRAs and 529 plans.

The truth about retail mutual funds, however, is more than concerning. Here are some of the key issues why assets are pouring out of mutual funds and into ETFs.

Spending Money to Make Money

Since their growth in popularity in the mid 1970's, mutual fund companies have made a fundamental change from originally putting the investor's profits first to now putting the company's own profits first. Kiplinger.com reports that the average domestic equity fund now spends an average of 1.4% of its assets annually on operating costs – almost twice what they were in the 1970's. International and specialized funds charge upwards of two percent or more on average. The best ETFs charge a fraction of these fees.

Despite the one percent or more in management fee that they charge, retail funds roundly underperform their respective benchmark in the long run. Standard & Poor's Indices Versus Active Funds Scorecard (SPIVA) reported that for the five-year period leading up to 2008, the S&P 500 outperformed 69% of actively managed large-cap funds. They also reported that actively managed small cap and large cap funds were outperformed by the S&P Mid-Cap 400 and Small-Cap 600 indices 76% and 78% of the time respectively.

On top of the operating expenses, mutual funds incur brokerage commissions on the huge volumes of trading that they do on an annual basis. According to Morningstar, these trading costs and other fees add an additional 1.2% in fees to the average mutual fund's costs.

As a general rule, ETFs have fewer types of undisclosed fees and they are generally less expensive to operate versus a mutual fund.

Finally, when buying shares of a typical mutual fund, you must pay a sales charge – depending on the class of share you buy. From no-load to Z shares, each load type is structured differently to confuse the average investor beyond being able to understand how much they are really paying for their investment. If you add them all up, the real cost of the average mutual fund (including no-load funds!) ranges from 2.5% to 4.5% per year plus approximately five percent in the first year for loaded funds.

By contrast, investing in individual stocks and ETF's will cost you only a fraction of these fees. The average ETF has an expense ratio of 0.44% and little to no trading costs because they buy and hold specific securities based on the objective of the fund – making ETF's up to 50 times cheaper than mutual funds.

Bottom Line: Mutual funds are expensive relative to the value they actually bring to the investor, and there are equally or better-performing alternatives that are less expensive.

The Elephant in the Room

One legitimate reason for a mutual fund to close the doors to new investors is that when a mutual fund becomes too large, it can no longer invest prudently to benefit the shareholders. As of March 12, 2009, the largest equity retail mutual funds topped $80 billion in assets each. With so much money under management, it becomes almost impossible for the fund managers to continue to find good investments that are large enough. When there are no more good investments, and there is additional money to invest, the only options left are bad options.

When mutual funds become this large, we often find a phenomenon known as "closet indexing." The annual management fee that you pay on a mutual fund as opposed to an exchange-traded fund is supposed to be a premium for the active management and trading of the fund. But instead of being actively managed, larger fund managers simply mirror the holdings of a benchmark index such as the S&P 500 or Dow Jones Industrial Average. Note: This is also one way that retail funds ensure that their returns aren't appalling as compared to a given benchmark index. It would be pertinent to note, however, that over 90% of indexed mutual funds underperform their benchmark index after fees.

To profit off the enormous success of a given mutual fund, fund companies will often release a version II of the fund. While the reproduction may or may not have the same objectives or risk tolerance as the first fund, the manager will almost certainly be different. With a different driver in the driver's seat, the two investment vehicles may perform very dissimilarly.

Bottom Line: Bigger isn't better when it comes to mutual funds. If it's popular now, chances are it already has its best years behind it.

The Revolving Door

You may be surprised to know that over half of all mutual fund managers have been managing their fund for less than three years. On the flip side, less than ten percent of managers have been managing for ten years or more. Maybe it's the stress of the job, or maybe it's that fund companies are quick to yank managers with a short stretch of sub-par returns. The results are two-fold for the mutual fund investor: inexperienced managers and high asset turnover. New managers will often sell the majority of the previous managers' investments and buy their own picks to prove that they are different – even though the previous holdings may be primed for a comeback. High asset turnover also means high transactional costs as well.

Most mutual funds are members of a larger family of funds created by a fund company. Because the company has a very large stake in its individual funds doing well, it is not uncommon for them to manipulate perceived returns by shuffling managers and even holdings among the funds to create all-star funds. A study by Robert H. Smith at the University of Maryland notes that "the dispersion in total portfolio risk in a cross-section of mutual funds can create the appearance of performance persistence, even when none is present." According to Morningstar, 60% of all mutual funds' purchases in 2006 went into 4 and 5-star funds. Clearly, there is a huge motivation for the fund company to produce highly-rated funds – sometimes through rabbit-out-of-the-hat illusions.

Mutual funds have also been known to obscure their actual performance. One tactic that retail funds sometimes use is to purchase successful or trendy stocks after they have already realized their maximum value. By doing so, the fund can publicize that they hold those stocks to attract uninformed investors. In most cases, these cosmetic purchases will take place shortly before the fund reports its holdings and statements are sent to investors.

What's more, such cosmetic portfolio changes cost the fund-holders significant amounts in transaction fees and tax consequences.

Morningstar.com is a great place to research the background of a mutual fund's management, simply by searching for the fund and clicking on Management. Of course, with an ETF you do not need to worry about management – only the holdings of the fund, which can also be found on Morningstar.

Bottom Line: The performance figures that a mutual fund advertises may not tell the whole truth.

A Taxing Issue

Many mutual fund investors are shocked to learn that, after coping with the losses they sustained through this market pullback, they may receive a substantial tax bill as a way of thanks. That's right—mutual fund investments are one of the only ways that you can actually be taxed on your losses.

"Phantom taxes," as they are sometimes called, are a lesser known—and less desirable—characteristic of mutual funds. Simply explained, as a mutual fund tumbles in a bear market, an unusually large amount of investors' cash out their shares. Fund managers have no choice but to sell securities to pay off the deserting shareholders. Inevitably, this event creates capital gains as long-held stocks are liquidated. Tax laws require mutual funds to distribute the net gains from sales to shareholders by year-end. The more investors that leave a fund, the more capital gains that can be unduly realized—and the bigger the tax burden for the remaining shareholders.

Long-term capital gains distributions can be taxed at a maximum rate of 15% as of March 15, 2009, while short-term capital gains a substantially higher rate. Over time, the average investment holding period has dropped from four years in 1980 to less than nine months today according to Morningstar. This translates to more than twice as much tax on realized gains. On the other hand, if you die the IRS allows a "step-up" in basis and no tax is ever paid on the inherited securities.

If you have a taxable account that holds ailing funds, do your research and explore your options. If you own shares on the distribution record date, you will be taxed. Distributions are generally made in mid-December and are published by the mutual fund companies beforehand.

Be especially watchful of many funds with high-flying trends over the recent history. These are the funds that generally experience the most capital gains on their underlying investments. To find the projected distributions of a particular fund, contact the fund company or visit their website.

Ethics Conflicts

Conflicts of interest have been the source of numerous corporate scandals over the past decade – including Enron, WorldCom, Tyco and others. In the case of mutual funds companies, their funds and their managers, conflicts of interest can lead to unethical decisions and loss for investors. One particularly disturbing example is that, according to the Wall Street Journal, there were 124 individual portfolio managers managing both retail funds and hedge funds as of 2007 – and those were just the ones tracked by Morningstar! Hedge fund investors pay their managers up to 20 times as much as mutual funds. With such an obvious conflict of interest, the problems for the fund shareholders abound.

Specifically, these managers can perform trades in the larger retail fund and then turn around and make hedge fund trades accordingly, to benefit off their inside knowledge. Or, a conflicted manager may even make unallocated trades – waiting until later to decide which fund he bought the investment for based upon how profitable it turns out to be – rewarding the smaller fund at the expense of the larger, more established fund. Unlike the Sarbanes-Oxley laws which largely address the issue of corporate conflicts of interest, the SEC does not dictate how to handle side-by-side managers' potential conflicts – and many fund companies even encourage these scenarios.

Your best alternative for active and trustworthy management is a fee-based advisor that does not make money from commissions or selling specific investments. Be sure that your investment advisor's incentives are tied to your objective: positive returns.

What's in a Name?

How many casual investors can look at a fund's current holdings and formulate an understanding of the risks and objectives of the fund? The reality is that without rigorous and unbiased professional help, selecting a fund can come down to selecting a fund purely by its name. While many mutual funds do invest 100% according to their goals and objectives, many experience a phenomenon known as "style drift" or "bracket creep" whereby they stray from their original classification over time. While occasional positive returns from this type of investment change are often attributed to the "flexibility" of the manager, the reality is that investors have chosen that investment for a specific role in their portfolio.

You have probably seen commercials or advertisements lately capitalizing on the "economic crisis" theme in order to have their product seem current or applicable in this economic period. Mutual funds have been known to try the same tactic by changing their fund name to reflect the trendy buzzwords of the time. In 2006 alone, Lipper Inc. reported that 719 funds "fiddled" with their names. A 2003 study also found that funds that modified their names attracted 22% more money than those that didn't.

Similar to name changes, mutual fund companies have been known to close and reopen funds for a variety of reasons. One is that closing underperforming funds boosts the company's overall fund family performance numbers. Likewise, new funds and funds that are closing draw investors based on their perceived (and marketed) scarcity and uniqueness. The common theme among these name-based ploys is that they profit only the mutual fund, not the individual investor.

An alternative to simply relying upon a fund name or description is to read a current, unbiased report on the mutual fund. Such reports are often available at www.MSNMoney.com or www.Yahoo.com. Finance.com by searching for the fund's ticker symbol. Even better, having a relationship with a professional advisor that you trust can be your most valuable tool to keen insight and impartial advice.

So that wraps up our version of Basic Investing 101. We discussed the six key concepts to investing, the essentials to effective diversification, asset selection and how broad investment categories work, the types of investment accounts, why we use ETFs over mutual funds allocation basics. If you were not ready to find out about investments that work, you are now. Please, use the extensively defined terms in the glossary if you come up with a term that you do not understand.

The rest of this chapter is not intended to offer investment advice, but to offer direction on where to get that advice.

In this chapter you will go from the theoretical to the practical, and learn specifically where to invest. Although this can be done in many ways, the wisest and safest way is to put yourself into the hands of an honest and savvy financial planner. It's not wise to rely solely on your own limited knowledge, nor is it wise to follow the advice of TVs financial experts, who tend to focus on short-term market reactions instead of long term.

Fortunately, you don't have to re-invent that particular wheel; you need only need to find a mentor.

- First, identify people who are successful investors, and have achieved their investment goals. You might find such people through your parents, or in your church, or through your university alumni association.
- Once you find them, ask them who their financial planners are.

- After you gather a half dozen or so names, go financial planner shopping.

- Explain your long-range objectives, and ask how the planner would recommend that you achieve them.

- Ask the planner what he would do and how you can hold him accountable to an unbiased index or standard.

- Have your chosen mentor help you compare each of their plans, and try to get a feel for the one with whom you feel the most comfortable, the one who seems the most committed to helping you.

James' experience with Brett Machtig

In order to show to his procedure works, let us return to James, whose financial plan was described in chapter six.

After completing his financial planner shopping, James selected the author of this book, Brett Machtig. He made his decision based on Brett's 30 years of experience, his thorough knowledge of the area, and most importantly, his genuine desire and commitment to seeing James achieve his goals.

At their first planning session, Brett didn't try to rush through the meeting and come up with a plan in the shortest time possible. Instead, he wanted James to have a broad view of where he is, and how to get to where he wanted to go. Brett asked a lot of questions to clarify James' vision, and then gave him s lessons on investing. Before he listed the lessons, Brett explained one of the most important concepts in his economic theory, a definition of wealth. His definition of wealth is the ability to live off the return of one's investment assets, while leaving the principal intact.

A wealthy person is one who can live comfortably without having to work; one for whom work is an option, not a necessity.

Six Lessons to Learn for Financial Freedom

Lesson 1: Have a Plan

Brett began by congratulating James for having created an 18-year plan. "Since you have already mastered this lesson, I'll simply make a few comments," Brett said. He explained that planning is everything—one starts at the finish line. That means you must see the end result before you start a new venture. If you can't see the end at the beginning, you'll have a hard time getting there.

For example, while you're still young and beginning your adult life, you need to see what life is like in old age, and then plan accordingly. As you begin college, find out immediately what your career goals require for a successful graduation, and work toward that goal from the start. It's a cliché, but still true: if you fail to plan, you plan to fail.

Brett explained that the greatest gift to give yourself is a life goal. Major life goals can be divided into financial, romantic, career, and spiritual. To make sure that your goals are not pipe-dreams, you must pin them down to a timetable, and slowly and logically follow your timetable. "It's easy for me to talk about planning," Brett said, "but hard for most people to do. If you go to any 20-year high school reunion, and ask those present if they fulfilled the dreams they had when they were 18, most would admit they haven't, but that they settled for something far less than they wanted. If questioned closely, most would have to admit that they had just lived day by day without any goal in mind."

Lesson 2: Spend Less Than You Make

Brett said James' 18-year plan showed that he had mastered the planning lesson. He praised James for living on a frugal budget, for saving at least 15% of his take-home pay, for refusing to buy a new car, and choosing not to rent a luxurious high-rise apartment. He said that James' frugality showed that he had avoided the "expenses rise to meet income" trap.

Frugality is a habit that becomes a guide when making large and small decisions. Smart small decisions add up to thousands of dollars over time.

As an example of spending less than you make, each year reduce vacation expenses by $500 by staying one day less, or driving instead of flying, or eating inexpensive meals. Then invest the $500 you save each year. By the time you're 65, it will amount to $263,503, assuming a 10% growth rate.

Or, consider buying a smaller home. Let's say this decision would cut your payments by $300 a month. If you invested $300 a month from age 30 to 65, at a growth rate of 10%, it would amount to an astronomical $1,138,991 at retirement. The idea is to live well but simply, and avoid extravagance.

Lesson 3: Stay out of Debt

James already agreed to limit his debt to his mortgage. Remember that every minute of every hour of every day, you have to spend money. Remember that what counts is what happens in the long run. In the long run, you must be financially free.

Lesson 4: Liquidity

Liquidity in terms of money means having immediate access to cash when, as the saying goes, "Shit happens." When it does, usually money is needed as part of the clean-up process, but that money needs to be separate from your regular savings, or your savings can be wiped out. Appliances malfunction, cars break down, accidents happen, sickness strikes. Although misfortune surprises us, you can plan for these emergencies:

A.   *Create a Rainy Day Fund. Put aside in savings or money market accounts a fund equal to three to six months of your average monthly expenses. That's to be untouched unless a major crisis happens. It won't do any harm sitting there earning interest, and if you need it, it will save you from having to run up large balances on your credit card, borrow from relatives or friends, tap into your investment accounts, or surrender the title to your car for a quick loan at exorbitant rates. As a single person, when life is less complicated—trust me, it is—it's easier to set up your rainy day fund, and be prepared for the curves that life throws.*

B.   *Carry Life Insurance*
Another way to protect yourself from life's curves is to carry life insurance. The cheapest kind is term insurance. As a single person, one does not need much coverage; just carry enough coverage to pay off debts and cover burial expenses.

C.   *Get an Umbrella Policy for your home and car, which takes over where your renter's policy and auto policy leaves off. For example, you can get a one million dollar policy for just $100 dollars a year. If someone slips and falls on your property, and sues you, it is very comforting to have this policy.*

Lesson 5: Harnessing the power of volatility.

Brett practices the Law of Buying Low and Selling High by balancing a portfolio at least once a year. As James gets more money to add to his investment portfolio, he should use the money to re-balance the portfolio at least annually. That's how a person buys low and sells high. For example, if James had $75,000 in his portfolio, he would start off with $25,000 in each third of the portfolio. After one year, due to investment growth and additional contributions, his portfolio now is $120,000. The real estate portfolio equity grew to $60,000, the stocks fell to $20,000, and the cash and bond portfolio grew to $40,000. James would move $20,000 from his real estate portfolio to his stock portfolio, rebalancing each portion of his investments to $40,000 each, and ready to start a new year.

Lesson 6: Harnessing the Power of Compounding

Compound interest is one of the greatest miracles known to mankind. The way it works is a little like the Big Bang theory. Just as the Universe started from something very small, and burst into something seemingly infinite, compound interest can start with a small amount of money, and expand into an astronomical sum, not as quickly as the Universe inflated, but over a long period of time. For example:

1.   *If you were given a dollar at birth, and were able to double that dollar every year, at age 18 you would be able to buy a home valued at $130,000.*
2.   *At age 22, if the rate were 10%, you'd be earning $200,000 in interest from your investments.*

3.   *At age 30, you could own a $1 million dollar home in over 500 cities worldwide.*

4.   *If a person wins $12 million in the lottery, and chooses the cash option, she will only receive $6.5 million, excluding taxes. However, if she accepts payments over a 20 year period, allowing compound interest to work its magic, she will receive the entire $12 million, excluding taxes. In addition, the lotto company will have earned enough interest on the same money to pay off the winner without having used any new money of theirs.*

5.   *Looking at the flip side of the lottery, the lowest income groups spend about $200 a year buying losing tickets. If they had invested that money at 8%, from age 18, it would amount to $196,068 at age 67, according to McKenzie and Lee in Getting Rich in America. These authors also encourage readers to bring coffee to work, and avoid Starbuck's. The savings, when invested at 8%, will amount to $282,700 by age 67. The same is true for avoiding junk food in vending machines. By age 67, one's invested savings would amount to almost $300,000.*
6.   *In an earlier chapter you were advised to avoid buying the entry-level Lexus ES 300 at graduation. If you buy a certified used car, and invest the $25,000 you would have spent on a new Lexus, it would amount to over $500,000 by age 67. Just because you're young, don't imagine that 67 is the end of life. Sixty-seven-year-*

olds are full of life. They start new careers, go on cruises, get married, and look forward to 20-30 more years of satisfying living.

7.   *Then there's "The rule of 72," in which you divide 72 by your interest rate of return. That figure shows how many years it will take to double your investment. Suppose you have $100,000, and you can make 6% interest. Divide 72 by 6, and you get 12; in 12 years your $100,000 will have doubled to $200,000. If you could get an 8% return on $100,000, you would divide 72 by 8, which is 9. At 8% your $100,000 would jump to $200,000 in nine years. The beauty of compound interest is that your money is making money, and you don't have to lift a finger. If you had to work for $100,000, even if you made $100 dollars an hour, it would take 1,000 hours.*

It's imperative to invest over the long haul, so compound interest can work its magic. Put it in and leave it in, don't get heartburn from the ups and downs of the market, and don't check your portfolio earnings each day. Don't panic when the market bottoms out, or when multi-billion dollar corporate scandals cause thousands of unwise investors to lose their life savings.

Investing over the long haul is best because the history of the stock market shows average earnings of 8-10%. In the short haul, these figures may go up or down, but over 20 years that market will average this return. What the market will do over 20 years is clear. What it will do day to day or year to year can't be predicted by Warren Buffet or Mark Cuban. So, diversify and don't worry, be happy.

Many ultra-conservative workers have put all of their assets in the company they work for. It worked out well for some of the lucky ones. At the 3M Company in Minnesota, the standard joke was that one must treat the old custodians courteously because their company stock had made them millionaires. Many retirees of the John Deere Company are living well after putting all their savings into company stock. However, they are the exception, not the norm. Thousands of others put all of their savings in one

company and have been wiped out by company fraud or
liquidation.

A Philosophy of Investing

Winding his informal session with James, Brett said again that
his goal was to help James formulate a philosophy of investing,
based on the time-tested philosophy of not putting all of your eggs
in one basket. This philosophy gives you peace of mind, knowing
that one or more of your "eggs" is in a state of growth, so that you
can be assured of a gradual path toward financial security.

Rewards of managing money wisely

We have seen examples of prudent people who have managed
their money wisely. We hope you feel enthusiastic about doing the
same. Let us tell you what it feels like to be financially free:
powerful, safe, confident, and self-assured. You have no debts,
and when bills come in the mail, you pay them on the same day.
You rejoice in knowing that you can send your children on
vacation anywhere in the world. You can afford to send them to
any school in this country or abroad, because money is not an
issue. When your children get married, you can buy a house for
them and let them make payments to you. You can finance them
if they want to start their own business.

When relatives or friends are in trouble, you can bail them out
immediately. When sound investment opportunities arise, you
will have the means to take advantage of them. You realize that
money is like a shield that protects you from the world's
harshness. Having money allows you to help those who cannot
help themselves. The three of us know of no greater joy than
helping others.

For example, a pre-school in Mamelodi, a township in Pretoria,
South Africa has 100 pupils and five teachers. While tuition is
only $13 a month, many parents don't have it. The teachers begin
their day at 6:30AM, and go home at 5:30PM. After the principal
pays the rent, the food bill for the children's lunches, and the

utilities, there's no money left for teachers' salaries; they are volunteers. After working 55 hours a week, they go home with nothing. Their love for the children motivates them to come back day after day, year after year.

A financially comfortable American visited the school one day and cried to learn of their situation. He learned that for just $1,000 a month, he could feed 100 children, pay the salaries of five teachers, plus the rent and utilities. Realizing he could do so much for so little, he began to send a $1,000 check to the school each month. No words can describe how this act of kindness makes him feel, especially when one considers that these people were victims of one of the most brutal governments of the 20th century, until their independence in 1994. Having money can help one make a difference.

While money can do many good things, it can't make you happy. Lionel Richie remarked that he went to a party where everyone was rich, and no one was happy. One man told him that, if he could be happy for one day, he'd give away all of his money.

Money is a means, not an end. Use it to improve the quality of your life, and to help others. Then seek complete fulfillment in the exploration and development of your inner self. Only there will you find lasting peace. Hindus say that humans are little sparks of a greater power. When you find your Source, you find yourself. Four of the greatest masters in the art of finding oneself are: Maxwell Maltz; Deepak Chopra, *Magical Mind, Magical Body*; St. Benedict, *The Rule of St. Benedict*, and Tony Robbins, *Unlimited Power*.

SUMMARY

1) Diversification is investing in such a way as to minimize your exposure from any one event devastating your nest egg. The acid test of proper diversification is whether the investment portfolio components move up or down at the same time.

2) Investments to consider for proper diversification include: (a) Fixed-income: Bank savings accounts, money market accounts, bank CDs, annuities and bonds (b) Stocks: dividend and growth, U.S., as well as international (c) Real estate: Rental, commercial, REIT, private placement (d) Limited Partnerships: Equipment leasing; apartments, offices, nursing homes, retail space, oil and gas.

3) Once you are diversified, practice buying low and selling high, or more accurately, know how to sell high, and then put the proceeds into the asset classes that are down. You do this by investing in different asset classes – fixed income, equities and real estate. A year later, each asset class responds to the economy.

By comparing each investment to its prior value, you will know if they have gone up or down. Then sell enough high assets and add to the low assets so you have the same amount invested in each.

4) By using expense accounts, income accounts, brokerage accounts, children's accounts, mutual funds and retirement accounts you can match the investment with the best place given your needs.

In the U.S., we are taxed for everything – income, property, inheritance, gains, luxuries, fuel, alcohol, sales, marriage and even hunting and fishing. By reducing your taxes, you are reducing one of your largest expenses.

V. THE KEYS TO REAL INCOME TAX REDUCTION

*J*ohn has a great insurance business in Minneapolis. He has been using the same accountant for five years. Each year, he brought his receipts to his accountant who then would calculate the tax. One day, John went running with me on a five-mile loop around a local Minnesota lake. It was just before sunrise, clear and temperatures were hovering around six degrees above zero. In the distance we could see the quiet skyline of Minneapolis about five miles away.

During the run, it became obvious that John was not considering all potential deductions. Key information was never collected that could have reduced his taxes. In addition, John waited until March every year to give his accountant the tax information he thought his accountant needed. By then, it was too late to consider John's best deductions, and too late to do things to reduce his tax.

I suggested using TurboTax® to collect the data and John was amazed at all the deductions he missed by not giving the accountant the information prior to year-end. Now, John makes decisions to change his tax liability before it is ever reported to his accountant or the IRS. John is more in control of his taxes.

Earlier in the book we mentioned that our experience has shown that most people who receive large sums of money lose it within three years.

Some lose it by spending the windfall. Some lose it by having poor cash flow and having their "faux investments" or non-producing assets consume the newfound fortune. Here we will talk about the other way people can lose large sums of money – by owing tax, interest and penalties to the IRS.

At the very least we will cover how to reduce your income tax bill.

For most Americans, tax preparation starts by bringing a box of receipts to a tax preparer or accountant. Then, the CPA prepares the return based upon the box of receipts.

Others prepare their own income tax returns, using the same "shoe box" process of adding up their income and deductions a month before the IRS deadline and paying the tax. Without professional help, many people are not sure they even know the right questions to ask to reduce their own taxes.

There is a better way. This chapter provides tactics and strategies to reduce your federal and state income taxes. This tax reduction comes not from some gimmick, loophole or "grey" tax area. Instead, it comes from doing a better job of gathering tax-related information, finding a great accountant, capitalizing on your best deductions before the tax year ends, and in being prepared for an audit.

> **Action Item:** Using a tax return program such as TurboTax, estimate your taxes before year end and run various scenarios according to the following tax-reduction strategies. Decide which strategies help reduce your taxes the most and implement those changes.

GOOD DATA COLLECTION

Have you ever heard the computer term, "garbage in, garbage out?" In programming language – the quality of the data out is only as good as the data entered. To do a great job on tax reduction, the first step is to ensure all related information gets in your return. We recommend using a tax preparation program like TurboTax®

to aid in data collection to ensure all deductions are considered and all potential tax reporting methods are reviewed.

For example, TurboTax® will walk you step-by-step through a tax interview process. The questions will address each possible tax issue or write-off. Tens of millions of dollars are spent on developing this program each year and it is very user friendly.

For personal use, Quicken does a great job of managing the in-flows and out-flows of money. For business tracking we recommend Quick Books as it offers more features helpful for small businesses taxes.

The program interacts with other useful software to help in data collection through valuing potential deductions of donations and property. One of these programs, "It's Deductible®," is useful in valuing non-cash gifts made to organizations like Goodwill and Salvation Army.

By using TurboTax®, you can run what-if scenarios on how different aspects of your taxes can be changed by small or bigger changes. For example, if you plan on living in your house for a while, you may be able to write off some of it for business expenses. What about selling your car? Again, TurboTax® will show you the foreseeable ramifications of such decisions.

TurboTax® does an excellent job of consolidating information but it allows the user to put income in the wrong places, thereby calculating the wrong tax liability.

It also does not handle basis calculation for small businesses, tax loss carry forwards, or K1 and small business tax returns. The average business owner would need a CPA to do these calculations.

On a personal level, with all my expertise and tax experience for both business and personal, I use TurboTax® for my data gathering and provide the completed tax return (and working papers) to my CPA. The final tax is never the same as I calculated.

If you buy TurboTax® before the year-end, you can see where you stand relating to your adjusted gross income (AGI), possible deductions, and approximately what your income tax liability will be before the year is over. This way you have time to change the tax, not just change its reporting. The whole interview can be done in a couple of hours and it will put you in control of the income tax process.

Once the basic information is entered and your tax is computed before year-end, you can work to change your taxes by considering tax-reduction strategies like:

- Adding to a retirement account to reduce taxable income
- If tax rates are low, you may take money out of a retirement account or convert to a ROTH IRA
- You can start a business
- Maximize your IRS Section 179 deduction, which allows you to expense capital purchases
- Sell mutual funds outside of your retirement plans and replace them with ETFs or individual stocks
- Deduct the costs of remodeling your basement by converting it into a home office
- Donate clothes, unwanted items, cars and property to approved charities, then, use the software program "It's Deductible®" to set a value for the donated items
- Take a loss or gain on investments
- Pay your property taxes before year-end
- Write off a bad loan, then send a 1099 to the person who would not pay so that the IRS becomes their new bill collector
- Pay next year's business-related expenses, before year-end
- Start a charitable foundation
- Look at special deductions, e.g., improving your energy efficiency can create tax savings in some cases

Bobbie is a competent, self-made success. He is very self-reliant and does his own taxes. He is also very philanthropic. Bobbie sat down with us for our quarterly financial review. We discussed his income, expenses, taxes and asset structure. Bobbie mentioned that he borrowed $500,000 from his private charitable foundation. He reasoned he would rather pay his own private charitable foundation interest than his bank.

I was concerned about this transaction and had a tax attorney look into it further. His assessment was grim.

As a matter of fact, the Internal Revenue Service (IRS) has addressed that particular scenario. If Bobbie paid off the loan within 12 months of the loan's inception, the penalty would be a small interest penalty only.

If, however, the loan was not paid within 12 months according to the tax attorney, the penalty would be two times the loan amount, plus an interest penalty from the loan inception. Had we not looked into this issue, Bobbie could have potentially owed the IRS more than $1 million dollars.

As I was completing a final edit on this book with my in-house editor, we came to this section. Through rereading my own work, I was able to work out a tax savings solution for one of my clients. I had just met with him at his multimillion dollar beachfront home, a property I had seen him construct just a few years before.

I was horrified to learn that the central air in the house was flawed, and as a result, there was mold forming behind many of the walls. The stress it was causing my client showed noticeably on his face.

Besides the strain of seeing his new house in disarray, his contractor was emphatically blaming the home owner—my client— for the problem. Regardless, the contractor was in the process of filing for bankruptcy, so he could not be a source of compensatory restitution for my client.

After rereading my own book, I found the most financially beneficial solution. My client spoke with his attorney and sued the contractor after all. Even though he was "drawing from a dry well,"

Action Item: Buy a copy of TurboTax®. Enter your data long before year end not to just calculate your tax, but to change your tax bracket. By using, you can be sure to know about all available deductions, as well as be able to run "what if " TurboTax® scenarios.

my client was able to write off the bad debt and send the contractor a 1099, effectively making the IRS his bill-collector. That year he was able to repair his house, and had a substantial tax deduction at year's end as a way of thanks.

HOW TO FIND A GREAT ACCOUNTANT

Have you ever heard about a person who represents himself in court? The attorney is an idiot and he has a fool for a client. The same thing may be said for doing your own taxes, for anything but the simplest of returns. If you are doing your own taxes, the only one who could catch an error is the IRS.

But how do you know if you have a great accountant?

A great accountant not only takes your shoe box of receipts to calculate your income taxes, she works to make sure clients provide the right information to her BEFORE the year is over. Then she does her own "what if" analysis.

She proactively works to minimize client's taxes through comprehensive income tax planning. Then, she goes to her clients with ideas to reduce both this year's tax returns as well as steps to take to reduce next year's taxes.

Compare this to an overworked accountant who just does the bare minimum to get by. He takes your information and enters it into his tax program. If you do not provide information, he does not ask. After populating the data he has, you get the completed tax return to sign, with no suggestions or discussions. The poor accountant provides no ideas to reduce taxes for next year. If you have a poor accountant, you need to find someone else to do your tax work.

Action Item: Find an accountant that will help make sure you give them all the pertinent data to produce a tax return at the lowest tax. This same accountant works on several "what if" scenarios and offers suggestion to reduce next year's taxes.

Steve loves his CPA, Mark. They have been friends since grade school. Steve trusts him in every way. Over the years, they have grown in their respective professions. Both are great at what they do. Mark moved to Minneapolis and Steve stayed where they were raised and started a manufacturing business. For most major decisions, Mark was there for Steve.

For example, Mark counseled Steve on business structure, how to minimize tax impact of a property sale, and where to get help for solving a complex business problem. That is how Steve and I met – to help Mark work out a complex problem facing Steve's business. Having competent people you trust is very important to Steve.

They openly discuss business partner issues, investment tax issues, cash flow, insurance, exit strategies, and bookkeeping. "Mark is not always right, but his perspective helps me make better decisions," relayed Steve. Mark is a great accountant.

How do you find a great accountant? The best way we know to do this is by asking mentors and other trusted advisors if they can recommend someone. Tap into your professional network who are good at what they do, and ask them who they look to for tax advice.

We also suggest pulling a tax attorney in to help in more complex matters like selling a business or looking at the cost and benefits of starting your own private foundation. By getting the right people on your tax team the rest of the chapter will be much easier to implement.

HOW TO LOWER YOUR TAXES

Now that you have gathered all the related data to complete your taxes and found the right CPA or tax preparer to help, let's explore ways to reduce your taxable income and increase your deductions.

AGI Income	Federal Tax	Tax Percentage
$ 131,451.00	$ 28,930.00	22.01%
$ 65,101.00	$ 10,638.00	16.38%

Reduce Your Taxable Income

Do you know how the IRS calculates personal income taxes?

It is based upon Carl Marx's theory of socialism, in his famous work, *Das Capitale,*

"To each according to his ability, to each according to his need."

The more you make, percentage-wise, the greater your tax burden will be, as a percent of your income.

All tax laws are subject to change for 2009 and in future years. Here are the rates for the tax year 2009, as of July 2008:

Filing Status and Income Tax Rates 2009		
Marginal Tax Rate	Single	Calculation
10%	$0-8,350	10% of the amount over $0
15%	$8,351-33,950	$835 plus 15% over $8,350
25%	$33,951-82,250	$4675 plus 25% over $33,950
28%	$82,251-171,550	$16,750 plus 28% over $82,250
33%	$171,551-372,950	$41,753 plus 33% over $171,550
35%	over $372,950	$108,215 plus 35% over $372,950
Marginal Tax Rate	Married Filing Jointly	Calculation
10%	$ -	$0-16,700
15%	$ 16,701	$16,701-67,900
25%	$ 67,901	$67,901-137,050
28%	$ 137,051	$137,051-208,850
33%	$ 208,851	$208,851-372,950
35%	$ 372,950	over $372,950

Our personal tax system is based on calculating Adjusted Gross Income or "AGI." If you lower your AGI, you lower the amount you are taxed, as a percentage of your income. For example, if you can lower your AGI from $131,451 to $65,101, assuming you are married and filing jointly, your tax goes down from $28,930 to $10,638. Your overall tax as a percent of your income drops from 22 percent down to around 16 percent.

The actual tax savings is even better.

If you receive Social Security, reducing your AGI reduces the tax effects on your benefits at certain income thresholds. The AGI sets the amount of deductions you can take.

Your AGI determines if an IRA is tax deductible. Your AGI determines what medical expenses are deductible. Your AGI determines what business and professional expenses can be deducted. Your AGI even determines what losses can be deducted or at what rate capital gains are taxed.

If your AGI is too high, your Social Security is taxed. You get the idea – reduce your AGI and you can reduce your tax percentage.

So, how do you lower your AGI? Here are three ways to do it.

1. Start a Business

Our tax code is built around the small business owner. Not only will owning a business allow you to write off all related expenses, but it also allows you to deduct portions of what you already spend money on now – like your home utilities, travel, cars and part of your actual home expense.

Select a business that does not add to your cost structure. Here are some clients who started a business based upon their skills and interests:

Sam and Elizabeth are retired. When they built their dream home it was with the longstanding plan that Elizabeth would have an art studio built within the home to work on her art, which had taken a backseat to Sam's career while raising the kids.

They added a separate studio, office and classroom. During the week, Elizabeth teaches art, works on commercial graphic design, and paints original paintings to sell at local art fairs. They set up a Limited Liability for the art business.

They were able to write off all costs related to the building and furnishing of the studio and office as well as the prorated share of their home utilities. They used IRS Section 179 of the tax code to expense the entire costs of $125,000 of their tangible personal property expenses for computers, etc.

They write off all materials and business advertising. They write off part of their automotive expenses. Lastly, they write off any other travel-related expenses in selling the art in fairs and exhibits. The write-off allowed them to reduce Sam's income tax so their Social Security was not taxed, as well as reduce the overall income tax percentage.

The art business is beginning to make money. Elizabeth is happy painting and they are living their dream retirement, while saving in income taxes along the way.

Because their overall AGI was lowered, they were able to write off a greater percentage of their other deductible expenses.

Steve had a great life, living in a sunny oceanfront community in southern New Jersey. He was young, healthy and wealthy, and did not have to work.

Then Steve had an idea. Using sophisticated personality profiling, he built a software program that could predict which salespeople would be able to perform and what underachievers needed to do to improve their effectiveness. If his company could predict which employees will do well, firms that use his services can do a better job hiring and training their people. Steve created the profiling business on a very small budget by using the expertise of former colleagues.

By working at home, Steve's business added to his quality of life, and gave him tax savings by writing off a prorated share of his home, utilities, business travel, direct development costs, and all the direct costs of making his home capable of operating his fledgling business.

During this time, Steve had very little income, so he was able to withdraw funds from his IRA and pay very little in taxes. The company should start making money in the next year or two, but in the meantime Steve's tax savings have already made the business worthwhile.

Jeremy lives in Orem, Utah and has purchased a building at a bargain price. Jeremy is in the highest income tax bracket. Jeremy follows our guidelines in buying cash flowing 10 percent property, based on his rents minus his costs, and divided by his property equity.

Because the property is depreciating, the property makes money for Jeremy, while reducing his taxes. When we met, Jeremy was invested in mutual funds that created income tax gains which forced his taxes higher, even though he reinvested his returns. Jemery even was taxed in years his mutual funds went down, because of "phantom income," or income caused by other mutual fund holders selling off the fund, which forces the manager to sell stocks to provide liquidity.

In short, the mutual funds added to his tax problems. I suggested moving his non-qualified mutual funds into individual stocks and ETFs that could be managed to reduce his taxes and selected stocks to be held long-term.

As long as he held the equity positions, Jeremy was not taxed on his gains. Lastly, Jeremy maximized a retirement account. Combined impact of these changes reduced Jeremy's taxes substantially, while increasing his passive income.

Is your home office small? By moving your office to a more spacious location within your home, you might be able to deduct the remodeling of a room or part of your basement, simply by moving your office there. Then, the increased home office percentage will help increase the write-off relating to home utilities, maintenance and other non-deductible expenses.

Here are some other common business-related write-offs (based on 2009 tax code):

- Write off the costs of starting a business
- Maximize your IRS Section 179 deduction, which according to CPA, Jim DuPont, you can expense tangible personal property up to $250,000 per year
- Expense travel related to the business
- Take a home office deduction, as well as a part of your utilities
- Write off part of your car if you use it for business
- Buy something you can write off for your business that will improve its income prospects while reducing income tax
- Remodel a basement, have a tax deductible home office, and deduct 100% of the costs related to the office remodeling project
- Buy a computer
- Write off some of your insurance costs
- Deduct interest related to the business

Action Item: Write down in your journal ideas of the type of business you could start. Think about areas that interest you. Your business should align with your personal interests rather than become merely a time-consuming tax reduction tactic.

Do you have a business now? If you do not, consider one that will be fun, and one that will not become a cash flow drain.

You have to be careful to structure your business as a profit-seeking entity, not just as a "hobby business." The IRS will not allow you any tax breaks from a business that does not have the intent to make a profit. Whether you actually do make a profit or not is irrelevant. According to Jim Chase, a former IRS agent, unless permitted under other Internal Revenue Code Sections, IRC Section 183, commonly referred to Hobby Losses and Expenses, the IRS denies deductions from gross income for activities deemed to be entered into not for profit.

Treasury regulations under IRC Section 183 provide some 20 factors, not inclusive, to weigh in making a determination whether the activity is entered into for profit. The IRS does not require businesses to make a profit. The *intent* to make a profit is the determining factor of whether or not the business is legitimate or not.

Write down in your journal business ideas that suit you. Do you like to travel? Start a travel agency. Like computers? Start an internet-based business.

2. Help Others and Yourself through a Charitable Donation

Most successful people have already learned the importance of giving. We have clients who give to their church, support their schools, help others less fortunate, support their community and support the arts. You can give your time, money or possessions.

The US Federal tax system rewards those who give.

Bill a long-time client told me a story for the fifth time – a story about an Ames, Iowa marketing professor who really changed his life direction more than 60 years before.

"Why don't you remember him by making a donation to the college in his name?" I suggested.

"That is just what I will do," said Bill.

Bill set up that private foundation and made it the beneficiary of his estate. One-third went to support his church; one-third went to support education; one-third went to support his community.

Bill began funding his foundation with highly appreciated stock. The foundation saved Bill on income taxes while he lived, as well as began funding a vehicle to keep giving long after his death. Now, each year, Bill's generous gifts continue to help his church, his community and helps promote education through scholarships.

Virginia likes to go walking every day over the same three mile path through her bayside community. One morning, Virginia asked if I could join her on her walk.

It was a beautiful morning. As we walked and chatted, we fed the turtles and the ducks, and later were just about to cross over the foot bridge back to her house when her cell phone rang.

It was one of her favorite people in the world, her grandson. Minutes before, she was telling me how at such a young age, this grandson was so appreciative of life.

As she took the call, immediately I knew something was wrong. I saw Virginia's face turn from light and airy, to horrified.

"Grandma, I don't want to die at seven. And when I am eight, I don't want to die then either," sobbed a quivering young voice. On the other end, the phone was given to Virginia's daughter. I heard snippets of the heartbreaking conversation...he has cancer...it has already spread throughout his body...the doctors give him only a few months to live...

Hearing the call wrenched my heart. Tears flowed freely as I held Virginia's hand in comfort.

Within months, this sweet little boy succumbed to the cancer and died. In his honor, Virginia started a private charitable foundation to help find a cure for the terrible disease that took her grandson. Out of the worst of possible circumstances, Virginia began a bastion of hope and help for other families to find a cure for the terrible disease. Within a few months of beginning the foundation, family, friends, acquaintances and strangers all began to contribute to the foundation.

My son, Jonathan was being selfish. He was three years old and was not sharing. So I went to a nearby drugstore and Jonathan was asked to pick out gifts. Then, we drove to a county nursing home to give them away.

At first, the nurses were annoyed with the disruption of their Sunday morning routine.

"Does anyone here need ....a card with a puppy on it?" I asked the nurse on duty.

She thought pensively about it and said, "Yes, Mary always asks for mail, but never gets any."

As we walked into Mary's room, we saw Mary just looking blankly into space. Jonathan walked up to this heavy-set ninety-plus woman who looked like she was waiting to die.

"I have a card for you," said Jonathan.

Mary instantly came to life, as if pulled out a trance, and gave Jonathan a long hug and thanked him.

Energized by Mary's joy, we went from room to room giving the trinkets.

When Jonathan pulled out the last gift at the bottom of the bag, a popular golden angel lapel pin, the nurse mentioned that Chuck, a retired bachelor from a small farming community south of Grantsburg, Wisconsin, had lost his old angel pin.

Perfect!

We walked to his room and Jonathan jumped on his bedside and said, "I have your angel!"

Chuck started to cry tears of joy while saying, "You found my angel, you found my angel!" Chuck, having been stripped of all his worldly possessions, felt like the angel was a symbolic connection with God.

It's funny, we went there to teach Jonathan a lesson on sharing, but we all got the lesson.

Since that time, we donate Christmas gifts to country nursing homes as a family to bring a little joy to the lives of our seniors, and a feeling of contribution in our own hearts. Not only does it provide a tax deduction but it brings joy to the people who have been forgotten and teaches our children the joy of giving.

In all the above examples, beyond the good that has been accomplished, the donors were able to write off substantial deductions. This is money that can be reinvest in even more benevolence.

As you can see, starting to give does not have to cost a lot of money. Young Jonathan started with a mere $20 bag of trinkets. In fact, many excellent donations cost you nothing, reduce your taxes, or unclutter your lives. For example you can:

- Donate a unused car to a charity
- Donate stuff in your attic using *Its Deductible* to value the gift
- Donate highly appreciated stock
- Donate land to a charity to reduce your holding cost and have a significant write-off
- Donate clothes that no longer fit
- Donate items for charity to auction
- Donate your time and help out. This will not reduce your tax, but still greatly helps the charity
- Name kids as trustees for your private foundation to ensure giving is part of their lives
- Leave it when you die because you cannot take it with you

Pull out your journal and come up with ways you can give back and reduce your taxes the same time.

3. Restructure Your Investments to Reduce Taxes

How your assets are structured can have a tremendous impact on your taxes. Here are some guides on simple changes you can make to reduce their tax impact. Consider the following strategies: add to retirement accounts, convert ordinary income investments into long-term capital gains or dividends, and avoid phantom taxes.

Add To Retirement Accounts: By adding more to a retirement account, you can significantly reduce your current year taxes. IRAs, 401(k)s, 403(b)s and qualified pensions make it possible to reduce taxed income and save money before you have a chance to spend it. The key is to match your savings habits.

There is a separate solution for good savers verses bad savers:

a. Bad Saver – If you historically spend all you make, the retirement account is your forced savings vehicle. For example, if your employer allows you to put away 15 percent in your 401(k), "max out" the contribution. Using the lessons of the chapter on Cash Flow, you will eventually improve your non-retirement cash flow and begin to save outside of your retirement accounts.

b. Good Saver: Many of these retirement programs offer matched funds, where the company will "match" your contribution. For example, if the company matches 100 percent of the first 5 percent, not only will this defer the income taxes, but you immediately double your money!

The disadvantage is that the retirement funds are later taxed at the highest possible income tax category – ordinary income tax rates. In this case, consider contributing just enough to retirement accounts to qualify for company matched contributions. To illustrate, if the company matches the first 3 percent with a 50 percent match, take the free money! Set your contribution amount to the match.

If you are a good saver, you may be better off reducing the retirement contributions to the matched amount. Then, you can use the increased cash flow to pay off debts or develop a portfolio outside of the retirement accounts where income tax rates can be as little as nothing.

If you are looking to maximize your retirement accounts, there are many options to consider. For example, according to the 2009 IRS Tax Guidelines, you can put up to 25 percent of your income in a Simplified Employee Pension (SEP), contributions can be as high as $49,000, or you can put up to $6,000 in IRAs if you are over 50 and your earnings are less than $105,000 (married, filing jointly).

Should you take money out of an IRA to pay off debt? If you spend everything you get, the answer is "No." Keep it in the IRA.

If, however, you have good savings habits, the answer is "Maybe."

Because of a low-earning year or a major loss, you'll be surprised at how little the tax impact could be.

When doing tax planning before year end, if you are in a low income situation, add withdrawals from your retirement account and see the tax. If it is acceptably low, you might be able to use the money to improve your cash flow.

How are you set up with regards to your retirement accounts? Write in your journal ways to reduce your income by contributing to a retirement account. If you are a bad saver with few liquid investments outside of your retirement accounts, contribute the maximum amount to your retirement account allowed by your employer. If you are a good saver, you might consider setting your retirement contribution to the company match, so you can build a greater amount of non-qualified assets. Lastly, if you have little or no income, this might be a good year for an IRA distribution.

> **Action Item:** Write in your journal ways to reduce your income by contributing to a retirement account. If you are a bad saver with few liquid investments outside of your retirement accounts, contribute the maximum allowed by your employer. If you are a good saver, consider setting your retirement contribution to the company match, to build up your non-qualified assets.

Convert Ordinary Income into Unrealized Gains: Many clients create tax problems and do not even know they are doing so. According to the 2009 IRS Tax Guidelines, ordinary income can be more than twice the tax of long-term capital gains or dividends.

By shifting out of investments that cause ordinary income taxes to those taxed as dividends or long-term capital gains, if your income is above $65,100, your taxes will be 15 percent of your income or long term capital gains.

Below are some (a) ordinary income items and (b) long-term capital gain and dividend income items.

a. What is taxed as ordinary income?
- CDs
- Money market accounts
- IRA/retirement distributions*
- Annuities**
- Taxable bonds
- Short-term capital gains
- Some mutual funds
  - * Penalties may apply
  - ** Tax is ordinary income on gains, not distributions

b. What is taxed as Long-term Capital Gains and Dividends?
- Long-term stock and ETF sales
- Some private placements
- Long-term ADRs sales
- Closed-end mutual funds
- Parts of business sale proceeds
- REITS
- Some business income
- Long-term property sales

The goal is to move as many of your assets from (a) to (b):

For example, if you have a $100,000 invested at 6 percent and you are in the 33-percent tax bracket, by moving to investments that create a dividend versus ordinary income you can reduce your tax by more than half from $1,980 to $900, excluding state taxes.

As a side benefit, you can also earn capital gains on many of the dividend-paying positions. If you hold them long-term, you pay the lowest possible tax on the gains as well. If you let them grow until you die, you pay zero, nothing, nada in income taxes!

If you own mutual funds outside of retirement accounts, many investors learn about phantom taxes. A phantom tax is where you may or may not have earned an income but are taxed anyway.

In addition, a long-term holder will still pay significant short-term gains because the average mutual fund holding period is nine month. This doubles an investor's tax, even if the hold period is long-term.

Harry purchased a growth fund in January 2000. By the end of the year, the fund was down 50 percent. When the tax information came Harry was shocked! He had both short-term and long-term capital gains in spite of tremendous losses.

When he called the fund, they informed him, "It is not a mistake."

The explanation provided was that the fund needed to sell lots of positions to meet the requests for distributions–causing both long— and short-term gains. Consequently, Harry lost money and was taxed on gains made in earlier years, before he was even in the fund.

Harry was very surprised to learn that most of his gains in a mutual fund he held for years had almost no unrealized capital gains. In spite of his buy and hold strategy, he had been paying tax distributions that the mutual fund passed through to their shareholders.

Our suggestion is to use actual stocks or ETFs instead of mutual funds for large investors in non-qualified accounts. If your non-retirement portfolio is too small to own individual stocks, consider some funds which are "tax-efficient" and are managed to reduce the tax impact.

Write in your journal a tax reduction plan done by reducing your AGI or Adjusted Gross Income as it relates to investment income. By reducing the tax created from phantom income and converting ordinary income into dividends, you can make a drastic change to your tax consequences.

Action Item: Write in your journal which investments are in the (a) list of investments taxed at the highest rates and how you plan on shifting them to the (b) list where they are taxed at the lowest rates (from pg. 127). Then, if you have funds that create phantom income, convert them to individual stocks or tax-efficient funds.

Other Taxes

We have many other taxes to consider minimizing. Here are a few other taxes and some reduction strategies for them.

State: Move or consider having multiple residences. If you minimize your federal tax, chances are it will also minimize your state income tax. If you have multiple homes, living longer in the state with lower state tax, in say, Florida versus New York, may save you a bundle.

Property: Challenge your bill by monitoring comparable properties and what their taxes are by having a real estate agent check them for you. All are public records. To set an idea of price change go to www.zillow.com.

Estate: The current estate tax rate is 45 percent. Prepare the right estate plan for your net worth as covered in the estate planning chapter. Having the right estate documents, asset titling and structure can save you a bundle upon death. Also consider state estates, as they differ greatly.

BE PREPARED FOR AN AUDIT

The IRS has more ability than ever to cross-check your returns. Here is a list of things to do to prepare for an audit:

- **Keep good records.** Keep all receipts and worksheets used to do your returns. If your accountant keeps them, get copies. Keep records for at least seven years.

- **Prepare very carefully and check your math**. Math errors are very common, especially if returns are prepared manually. Math errors can cause an audit.

- **Send a representative.** If possible, send an accountant to keep the audit scope limited. Have them take backup documents and relevant worksheets.

- **Consider your answers carefully.** How an audit ends up may affect future years, if there is a problem.

Remember Bobbie from the beginning of this chapter? After pointing out the penalties he promptly paid off the loan.

So by being prepared, proactive, informed and by receiving good advice you can enjoy real tax reduction. In the next chapter we will address how to protect what you have.

> **Action Item:** Follow the steps above to either avoid an audit or deal with one in the event that it happens.

SUMMARY

1. There are numerous ways to reduce your taxes. The first step is to be prepared before the year is over and use TurboTax® to help you collect all relevant data

before the year ends. Then, run "what if" tax scenarios before you meet with your tax advisor and have her come up with tax reduction ideas now and for next year. TurboTax® has limitations in calculating business returns, loss carry forwards, depreciation, and basis for businesses.

2. Give all your support data to a competent accountant to make sure you did the return correctly. Expect the accountant to offer ways to reduce taxes in the future. Having a personal board meeting with your investment advisor, tax advisor and business mentor can improve your finances in general and your taxes in particular.

   With a tax advisor, you gain one more set of eyes to catch a mistake before the IRS does. It also gives you representation if there is a problem.

3. Consider different ways to change your taxes: start a business before the year is over; donate; add to a retirement account; or if your income is very low and you save regularly, consider an IRA distribution.

4. Be prepared for an audit.

5. Reduce other taxes like state, property and estate taxes.

No one needs insurance until they NEED it. Like when the storm comes and wipes out your home, a freak accident cripples your back, or illness puts you into a nursing home for life. Plug up the hole in your financial boat instead of letting it be the "key flaw" that sinks your ship before it can come in.

VI. PROTECTING WHAT YOU HAVE

*S*uzanne had it all—an exceptional life, two beautiful young children, a hard-working, successful husband and a terrific start to becoming debt-free with a portfolio worth almost $200,000, as well as owning part of a business and some real estate.

Their goal of being debt-free started eight years ago when Lois and husband Rick, her college sweetheart, turned 30. After eight years of hard work they were down to their last $50,000 of debt after paying off their student loans, cars, credit card debt and finally, their home.

Rick was a runner and took pride in taking care of his body. He believed the best form of insurance was taking good care of mind and body. They talked about getting insurance with our company. It was on their "To do" list.

When the tech bubble blew, Rick began a small start-up company. The pay was excellent, but they did not have the benefits of his larger employer. Work was stressful. Six years after starting the business, their hard work began to pay off. The company prospered and grew.

All aspects of their life began to align. Out of the blue, Rick began having increasingly frequent headaches. They went to a specialist and got the news that Rick had an inoperable brain tumor. The doctor gave him less than a year to live.

All Rick could think about was how his wife and two beautiful strawberry blonde girls could live. His business partner always handled the sales and it was his job to handle the operations. Who would run their growing company?

Unlike their personal finances, the business still had considerable debt.

You need to have certain bases covered, even if you have not developed your wealth to be able to self-insure. In this chapter, we will cover the topic of insurance, and how to protect your family in the case of loss. Your insurance needs change as you go from having a few investments to being truly wealthy. Consequently, your insurance should be reviewed at least once a year.

INSURANCE NEEDS CHANGE

Before you have significant assets, even a small setback can be devastating. Think back to your first car as to how overwhelming things seemed when your car broke down and you did not have the money to fix it. Later, when you were newlyweds, living on more love than money, you needed coverage for cars, home, health and disability with very small deductibles. At the time, small deductibles cost more, but it was so much better to pay a little now to cover losses you could not afford to take.

As you develop emergency funds, your insurance needs change. For example, as you build up a rainy-day fund, you might be more comfortable with larger deductibles in order to save on insurance costs. As your investment portfolio grows and your kids get older, you may need less life insurance. Your needs for disability insurance take care of times when your ability to work changes without notice.

As you near retirement, you may want to buy a long-term health care policy because the high costs of a nursing home might leave your spouse without funds to get by.

As your net worth grows into the millions, life insurance needs change again, so your estate does not need to be sold to pay for estate taxes that hover at 45 percent. In this chapter, we will review the key insurance coverage you need and what to look for in long-term healthcare, life and other insurance considerations.

LONG-TERM HEALTH CARE

Audrey and Gus loved each other and had just celebrated their 40th wedding anniversary. They were high school sweethearts who had met at their junior prom. While with other dates, as they danced, their eyes met. Gus explains with a childish grin, "I just knew Audrey, with her bright brown eyes, was the one." Three kids and a lifetime of experiences later, we sat down with them.

Gus was scared and Audrey was mad. For years he'd bragged about all the money they saved in long-term health care and life insurance premiums. Now, two weeks ago he was diagnosed with prostate cancer and the treatments were eating away at all their savings. Audrey was afraid of losing her lifetime friend and of living her golden years broke and alone.

You need two things to purchase insurance: health and money. Long-term care insurance exists to protect our assets. Life expectancy has increased and diseases that used to kill us now disable us. In fact, our last six years might not be that different than our first six years – just lived in reverse, being dependent, needing help bathing, dressing, eating and eventually, help wiping your own bum. The likelihood of having a long-term disability increases as our life expectancy increases and assistance may be necessary to care for ourselves as a result of old age, sickness or injury.

While the cost of insurance is relatively small, the cost to provide the care is not cheap. According to a study by the MetLife Mature Market Institute in October of 2008, the national average annual cost for a private nursing home care was $77,380 per year, or $212 per day.

While that is bad, it will only get worse, because health care costs far outpace inflation. This is noteworthy because typically a person will buy this coverage in their fifties and sixties to use the insurance in their seventies and eighties. At five percent inflation, costs double in 15 years. Therefore, if the average nursing home cost $77,000 per year, at 5 percent inflation, that coverage will increase to $160,000 per year. To compound the problem, the average stay is two years.

How are you going to pay for this help if you need it? You could:

- Rely on family and friends for care
- Rely on government programs, like Medicaid to pay
- Pay for it out of your assets or income
- Use a long-term care insurance policy

Let's consider each option: First, relying on friends, family or a spouse can be disastrous. Unfortunately, when you need them, they might not be able to help. Your family might also not have the desire to change your bedpans, or your requirements might cause undue stress in their lives.

Second, for many, Medicaid is the only option, either because you can't qualify for long-term care insurance due to medical reasons, or you can't afford the premiums of a long-term care policy. The disadvantage is this: you have to be broke to use this option. Given the nature of this book, this also is not a serious option.

Third, some have no choice but to self-insure. If you do not want to be a burden on your family or spend down your accumulated wealth, using your own assets may be your only option, but it can be a tremendously expensive one. Quite possibly, all your assets could be wiped out, leaving nothing for your spouse to live on.

Fourth, if you have good health and can afford the premiums, long term care insurance might be your best option. Not everyone, however, is a suitable candidate for this type of insurance even if they want coverage.

Here are a few examples:

- It might be too expensive, given your income. One guideline is to not spend more than seven percent of your income on a policy. Some families have their kids pay the premiums. That way, the kids will not have to provide the physical care but still can financially help out.

- If your net worth is less than $50,000, you are better off not owning the insurance and relying on Medicaid or other government assistance.

- And lastly, you need be healthy enough to have a policy issued.

For people with good health and the means to afford the premiums, long-term health care insurance is the most effective means to provide funds for care.

So how much does it costs? One healthy 55-year-old client who purchased a $5,000 monthly benefit, payable over a five-year period, with a 5-percent inflation hedge and 90-day waiting period paid premiums of $1,967 per year from a leading insurance company (for illustrative purposes only). While that may seem expensive, remember – if the insured needs care today, the policy would have a $300,000 benefit limit. If the care is needed 20 years from now, the benefit limit increases to $835,860.

In selecting a long-term policy consider companies with excellent ratings and a strong history of issuing long-term policies.

Make sure that you select a reputable company specializing in long-term care insurance and that your agent knows what he is doing. Determine whether the policy covers both nursing home care as well as in-home care, which runs about half the cost and may be better suited for your lifestyle. Also consider an inflation adjustment rider. The insurance coverage can run from a low of $50 to $250 per day and a policy can cover from as little as one year in a home up to a lifetime of coverage.

Discounts are available from most companies if you buy with your spouse.

> **Action Item:** Review your long-term health care insurance needs.

EVALUATING LIFE INSURANCE

We are living longer. In 1940, a male could expect to live to 60.8 years and a female to age 65.2. In 2004, the life expectancy increased to 75.2 for men and 80.4 for women, according to the U.S. 2000 Census Data. The good news – this longer lifespan can translate into lower premiums for life insurance, particularly if your policy is three years old or older, you could probably reduce your life insurance costs in a new policy.

How do you know if a policy is right for you? Here are some questions to help you find out if your policy should be updated:

- Do you have enough cash flow to pay the premiums?
- Is your policy a good investment?
- Is the policy with a good company?
- Have your needs changed?
- Has your net worth dramatically changed?
- Have you paid off the mortgage?
- Have the kids grown?
- Do you now have estate issues?
- Have your beneficiary needs changed?

Unfortunately, the many types of life insurance out there make finding the right kind confusing. Below is a brief explanation of several main types and when they may fit.

Term Life Insurance

Term life insurance has a guaranteed face amount or death benefit. Depending on the type of term policy the premiums may be guaranteed not to change for as short as one year, or as long as 30 years. In the early years, from ages 20 to 50, term insurance requires a lower cash outlay to maintain the coverage. In later years, term premiums can become very expensive or not be available at all if your health declines. Some term policies have an option to convert to a permanent policy while still being lower in premiums early in the policy.

Gary bought a term policy that had a premium guaranteed not to change for 20 years. He figured he would not need the insurance after 20 years. Now, 20 years later, he has diabetes and no insurance company will insure him. He has children in college and investments that didn't work as well as expected. He still needs the insurance and cannot get it.

So what should you consider in a term policy? Consider policies that offer a conversion to a permanent policy down the road, also consider a policy with a guaranteed renewal option. In short, be sure the term period ends when your needs end, not before.

Whole Life Insurance

Whole life insurance has a premium structure that guarantees the coverage, a death benefit and locks in the premium. Most accumulate a guaranteed cash value and the face amount. Whole life insurance is permanent insurance, meaning it is designed to be in force for the insured's entire life.

Peter bought a $10,000 whole life policy when he was 21, in 1968. At the time, his premium was about $15 per month. "That was a lot for me then," Peter explained, referring to the premium. Now, 40 years later the policy is paid up. The death benefit has grown to over $25,000. His dividend check this year is almost $600 and his cash value has grown to almost $17,000.

However, Peter never looked back to see if the policy fit his current needs. Now, with $200,000 in mortgage and credit card debt, his

$25,000 insurance value could not help much. Peter said, "I wish I would have purchased a larger policy."

What do you look for in a whole life policy? We suggest making sure you have the right amount for your needs. Consider selecting a good mutual life insurance company. You may receive dividends, which can be used to increase the face amount and cash value.

Make sure you check your policy to see if it is funded for your life or if it will run out of cash and require additional premiums to keep it in force. If the policy is being used to fund retirement benefits, monitor the cash value performance. Dividends change yearly and interest credited can change quarterly.

Lastly, do not get into the trap of borrowing from the policy for it will cannibalize the policy—it could die before you do!

Universal Life Insurance

Universal life insurance was created with flexibility in mind. The premiums and face amount can be changed by the insured, subject to evidence of good health. This allows the insured to build as much or as little cash value as they desire. Universal life insurance is also a permanent insurance – meant to last for your lifetime.

What should you look for in a universal life insurance policy? The biggest issue we see is ensuring the policy is on track, by requesting an in-force illustration. Many policies are sold at much higher cost structures and higher predicted investment returns than is likely to be generated. As a result, your policy may require substantial cash outlays by you to pay out the death benefit sold originally. We suggest checking these policies at least every couple of years, comparing the predicted cash accumulation to the actual cash values. If they begin to separate, look for a different policy.

Variable Life Insurance

Variable life insurance can be structured like whole life or universal life. The key difference is that the cash value is invested in mutual fund sub-accounts. The insured or policy owner chooses the mutual funds to invest in from a list of options provided by the insurance company.

Jim is a successful investor, maxing out his 401(K) plan, who did not qualify for a Roth IRA because of his high income. He purchases a variable life policy and contributes the maximum premium allowable every year. Jim manages the mutual fund sub-accounts and likes the tax advantaged growth he receives in the policy. Jim plans on using this to supplement his retirement income tax-free.

There are several key things to look for in a variable life insurance policy. First, be sure to reevaluate the investment performance of the sub-accounts in the policy. Second, work with your investment advisor and insurance professional to evaluate and monitor the asset allocation strategy. Third, we suggest checking these policies at least every couple of years.

Joint Life Insurance Policy

Joint life insurance, also referred to as Second-To-Die insurance, is useful for estate planning. Typically, a couple will acquire one policy covering both their lives. When the first spouse dies, the policy may still require a premium to keep it in force until the second death. At the death of the second spouse, the face amount is payable to the estate. Under current tax law, this policy works perfectly for paying estate taxes, which are due nine months after a person dies.

Bill and Marion are 65 years old and have a $20 million estate. They want to pass along as much of their estate to their children and grandchildren as possible. In working with their insurance professional and attorney, they came up with a strategy to pay the $5 million estate tax bill that will be due at the second spouse's death using a joint life insurance policy. The policy was placed in an irrevocable trust (ILIT) to remove it from the estate and fulfill its purpose.

What should you look for in a joint life policy? First, if the policy is not put outside the estate using an ILIT trust you will be adding to your estate tax problem.

For example if you have a $5 million estate and a $2 million insurance policy, your estate taxes would be almost $1 million more than if it were in an ILIT trust.

In other words, you can either cut premiums down substantially or increase your coverage just by putting the life insurance proceeds outside of your estate for the same cost.

Write in your journal what insurances you have and the types of insurances you need. Have each reviewed to make sure they meet the intended purpose. If you need help, go to our website at www.brettmachtig.com or call your advisor for help.

We will analyze a policy you are considering and its appropriateness for you and your situation.

> **Action Item:** Review your life insurance needs, and which types best fit your requirements.

Other Insurance to Consider

Disability Insurance

Disability insurance pays you up to 70% of your income, income-tax free if you are unable to work due to sickness or injury. Consider the value of being able to earn a living. A 35-year-old earning $100,000 per year will earn $3,000,000 by the time he is 65, without inflation (with 3 percent inflation those earnings top $4,900,000). Your ability to earn and work is your most valuable asset.

Tom is a successful architect with a group disability plan through his employer. After a careful review, we find that it only replaces 30 percent of his income. Tom purchases supplemental individual disability income insurance that brings his total income replacement up to 70 percent.

Since disability insurance is paid tax-free, we feel it will replace enough income to maintain his lifestyle. This individual plan allows him to replace the group coverage if he leaves his current employer and allows him to increase his coverage if his income goes up. The premium payments had to be paid by Tom, the employee, not the employer.

Action Item: Review your disability insurance needs.

Umbrella Insurance

This is the insurance that covers your umbrellas – just kidding. Umbrella insurance extends the liability coverage on your auto and home insurance. Typically, your auto policy will have liability coverage of $100,000 to a maximum of $300,000 per occurrence, per claimant. Umbrella coverage protects you from damages that extend *beyond* your regular policies. It is called umbrella coverage as it extends the limits of liability on all your property/casualty policies – home, boat, snowmobile or automobile, protecting your assets from lawsuits.

Joe was involved in an automobile accident and killed two people. The judge ruled against Joe to the tune of $1 million. His auto policy paid up to his limit or $300,000 of the claim. Who paid the balance? In Joe's case, his umbrella covered the additional $700,000.

Without an umbrella policy in place, this $700,000 balance would come from his personal assets or his wages would be garnished until the debt is paid.

Umbrella policies typically are available in $1 million increments and are surprisingly inexpensive. Most often, you can add a $1

Action Item: Review your umbrella insurance needs.

million of coverage for less than $500 per year. The rates depend on your diving record and whether you have teenage drivers in your home, to name a few examples. As with all insurance policies, there are exclusions. Always review the fine print.

Health Insurance

Health insurance is another vital coverage to have in place. Either you get this coverage through an employer, or you can buy it as a standalone policy. With an employer, the coverage is typically guaranteed issue, so preexisting health issues will not come into play.

Action Item: Review your health insurance needs.

Home Insurance

This insurance covers your home and its contents against damage or loss. Be sure to set a replacement value for all scheduled items, because "replacement" is all they will pay. Some of the things that are surprisingly not covered by most home insurance policies exclude claims by home laborers like cleaning staff, contractors or lawn care providers you have in and around your home regularly. Be sure to sit down with your home insurer and know what is covered and what is not.

Also consider having your home, auto and umbrella policies with the same agent so you have one person to go to when making a claim. Lastly, do not make small claims as they can raise your premiums or may even make you uninsurable. Do not cut premiums by waiving storm insurances unless you can afford to pay for the damages without losing it all.

Action Item: Review your home insurance needs.

Auto Insurance

Auto insurance covers your car and those injured in an accident. Sit down with your agent to make sure your coverage is adequate. The best way to reduce costs for auto insurance is to have a good driving record; encourage your children to strive for the Honor Roll and to not submit claims for minor damages or minor theft.

Action Item: Review your auto insurance needs.

Insure Your Investment or Its Cash Flow

Many people will insure their health. Most will insure their car and house. Why not insure a portion of your investment portfolio?

Some annuities will insure against loss. For example, one annuity contract offered by Allianz Life guarantees the highest account value, ten years prior. If the value goes up, owners get the increase. If the market value is lower, US Allianz will increase its guarantees to the highest point it was on its anniversary ten years before.

This type of investment allows investors to be fully invested in the market while limiting their downside risk. Contract owners are able to participate as markets move up, while limiting risk as markets move down. This is not an offer to buy or sell securities, please read prospectus before considering any insurance, not appropriate for all investors. Annuity products change very frequently and may not always be available to the public.

Other annuity contracts ensure cash flow. For example, the Prudential Life and River Source Annuities offer up to 6 percent distributions for life (as of May, 2010), plus the opportunity for increases as the principle increases. This is not an offer to buy or sell securities, please read the prospectus before considering - not appropriate for all investors.

Remember Rick? Rick did address the insurance before it was too late. About a year before the discovery of the cancer, they purchased a $2 million term policy. Rick had set up a buy-sell agreement and funded it with two $1 million policies.

Rick's wife Lois didn't remember much about the next nine months. Her days filled with hope, despair, worry, and finally, acceptance. Rick lived until four days after their youngest daughter Katie's fourth birthday. His last words to Lois were, "I love you and the journey we had. I will see you later on the other side." With that, he closed his eyes and died holding Lois's hand.

After Rick's death, Lois did have lots of things to worry about. At least money to pay the bills was not one of them.

We know insurance is rarely a popular topic, but hopefully you can appreciate the importance of protecting what you have. Our next chapter will address how to pass on your wealth without giving your kids' inheritance to Uncle Sam.

SUMMARY

1. Make sure you have carefully considered long-term health care, life insurance, disability, home, health, umbrella, car and investment insurance.

2. As your net worth and savings increase, consider increasing your deductibles.

3. Bid out each of your policies regularly to ensure you have the best rates at least every two years.

4. Keep your claims to a minimum as even a small claim can significantly increase your future premiums and, in some cases, lead to non-renewal of your coverage.

5. Keep your health. Not only will this make life more enjoyable, but eating well, not smoking and getting rest will reduce your insurance costs. If you need to lose some weight or stop smoking, get coverage now. Then, once you lose weight or stop smoking re-price your coverage.

6. Consider where you live as it impacts insurance costs. For example if you live near the ocean, your insurance premiums and uncovered damage from a hurricane could be extremely expensive.

7. "Insure your umbrellas, especially if you live in windy, rainy areas."

protecting what you have

*Good estate planning makes sure your assets go to those
you want, with the least possible estate tax, and in a way
that protects your heirs from asset loss due to divorce and
financial irresponsibility.*

VII. ESTATE PLANNING MADE SIMPLE

*L*ily has been divorced for a long time. It was truly like the
old movie "War of the Roses" with Michael Douglas and
Kathleen Turner. By the time they were done, they split
the assets evenly – half for them and half for the lawyers. Lily
learned two things: she hated her former husband and she hated
attorneys.

So, she decided to put together her own estate plan instead of using
an attorney. She went to the library to get a sample will. It was
really simple with only one son: she transferred all her assets to her
son, LeRoy's name.

LeRoy was not the model son. In fact, Lily was constantly bailing
him out of trouble. He was mostly unemployed and had a nasty
habit of parking his orange-flamed Harley-Davidson soft-tail in her
dining room (Yes, big bad LeRoy was living with mom at 43 years
old). I'd see him occasionally sitting on the couch sucking down a
Pabst Blue Ribbon dressed in biker gear watching TV as I met with
his mom about her investment portfolio.

She thought her estate plan was completely handled. Then her
son died from an untimely heart attack. Lily was devastated. If
losing her only son was not hard enough, she quickly learned that
her son had no will, and now her assets were in Leroy's name—
including her home.

Ever wonder who gets the money when someone does not have a
will? Their assets go to the next of kin.

LeRoy's next of kin was his mother AND his father. Needless to
say the prolonged legal battle that ensued ate up much of the funds.

WHAT IS ESTATE PLANNING?

Estate planning is the plan by which your assets transfer to your heirs with the least amount of tax and problems. The documents to do this may include wills, trusts, durable powers of attorney, health care directions, buy-sell agreements, foundations and family limited partnerships.

Here is a brief description of each one:

- A **will** is the basic document to settle your estate. It is simple and easy to create, but it can create estate issues, namely probate, on your assets. It makes all your financial affairs public, is costly and takes a lot of time to contest. The will specifies who will handle your affairs upon your death.

- **Trusts** come in many shapes and sizes. They are used to reduce estate taxes, keep financial information private and to address transfer problems, if there are heirs. Common trusts include AB Trusts, Insurance Trusts, Special Needs Trusts and Beneficiary Trusts. Trusts can be revocable or irrevocable.

- **Durable power of attorney** allows another to act upon your benefit and can be cancelled or recalled at any time by the grantor. The durable power of attorney becomes unusable upon the person's death.

- A **Health Care Directive** specifies what you want to happen if you need extraordinary efforts to keep you alive. It also specifies your organ donation wishes as well as whether you want to be cremated or buried. The health care directive also specifies who will be making these life decisions on your behalf.

If you have an older document this may be called "a living will" which is a sign that your whole estate needs to be reviewed because of changes in the law.

- **Buy-sell agreements** specify what will happen to a business interest if a person dies, gets disabled, wants out or retires.

- **Family limited partnerships**, as well as other advanced tools are used to maximize the transfer of assets while minimizing state tax consequences.

- **Private Charitable Foundations** are used to take a larger charitable deduction at the time of funding, limited to certain income tests. Then future charitable gifts can be paid through the foundation. Another benefit allows for reasonable compensation to its trustees who can be specified as your family, heirs or other interested parties.

> **Action Item:** What estate issues exist in your life? Are there complicated beneficiary situations or family-owned businesses? Identify areas that you should discuss with an attorney and advisor.

For them, the trustee compensation could be income.

What Documents Do You Need?

The documents that you need differ, depending on the size of your estate.

Under $1 million

For most, a will, a health care directive and a durable power of attorney is all you need. Make sure you include insurance proceeds in your net worth calculation. Make sure your heirs also have their wills in place.

Lance, 48 years old, is a divorcee from Detroit, Mich., with one daughter, Jena and not much else. After the divorce dividing the assets equally between his former wife and the attorneys, all that was left for him was some personal belongings and an IRA worth about $125,000. In addition to the IRA assets, Lance has a $1 million insurance policy.

Lance's attorney suggested an estate plan that was made up of a simple will, leaving all his assets to his parents, then in trust for Jena. His durable power of attorney is his brother Brady, who helped him through his divorce.

Lance's emergency contacts are Brady, then his parents, and finally his ex-wife, Joanne. His ex-wife will be Jena's guardian. Lance is rebuilding his life and his estate plan covers his needs for now.

$1 - $5 million

In addition to the will, health care directive and durable power of attorney, larger estates may need an insurance trust also known as an ILIT Trust and a trust to increase the estate tax credit. The biggest problem most attorneys see here is naming children as direct beneficiaries. They suggest leaving assets in a trust for children rather than direct gifts because divorce is so prevalent. By keeping funds in trust for children, the gift will survive any divorces the kids may have and may offer some protection against financial irresponsibility as well.

Amy and John are in the sunset of life. Their kids have grandchildren of their own and their lives are quieting down. They moved from their Bloomington Minn., neighborhood of 40 years to a senior condo and have a nice portfolio.

Their estate is worth $3 million and they have used an AB trust to eliminate any estate tax. Their durable power of attorney names their son Mark, who lives six miles away. Mark checks on them *often and shares the same accountant and financial advisor, "If I were to die, Mark knows just what to do," said Amy.*

"We even have three color dots (yellow, blue and red) on the back of our furniture and other assets, so each child knows what they will get. Luke, our youngest, even made copies of the family photos in digital form and sent them to his siblings. Sara will get mom's ring and as far as the financial assets, those will be split evenly three ways.

"If one of our children dies before us, then their portion will pass to the children of that child. Our burial plots have been selected and they even know where we want obituaries to be submitted. We tried to take the guess work out of what to do, to make it easier on our family. We have added Mark as signatory to our checking account as well. We had a great life and want to help our family. Every year we give to each child and grandchild some money to help them while we are still around."

$5 million or more

In addition to the tools used for a $1 to $5 million dollar estate, these larger ones may use family limited partnerships, private charitable foundations, Grantor Retained Interest Trusts (GRITS) and the other sophisticated tools to minimize estate tax.

Grayson is a southern gentleman who knows how to make his guests feel welcome. Originally from Plains, Ga., Grayson was a personal friend of former President Carter's family. Professionally, Grayson fixed broken companies for the Peste Companies. He became part of a mentor group almost 30 years ago.

And 30 years later, the group still meets and continues to do deals together. "I'm the poor one of the group, with a net worth of $20 million," said Grayson. He has been working on his estate plan for some time.

Grayson's wife of 25 years passed away after the AB trust was funded. That irrevocable trust now has assets worth $4 million.

His homes were transferred to his children over a 10-year period of time using a Grantor Retained Interest Trust (GRIT). A *foundation was established for his church and community support. The rest of his assets were placed in a family limited partnership, which transfers interest of roughly $10 million in assets to his children, creating an estate tax of $3 million. That tax is paid from an insurance trust using a $5 million paid-up life insurance policy. Grayson's attorney and accountant are some of the best. Still, their work is cross-checked annually by different attorneys and accountants.*

As you can see, the complexity of an estate plan changes the documents required. Also, the more complex your situation, the more important your counsel.

Action Item: Referring to your list of estate planning issues, what documents best address these issues? Write them down and make sure to follow up on having them created for you.

SELECTING AN ATTORNEY

How do you know whether or not your attorney is good at what he or she does? In managing money for decades, here are the guidelines we use in selecting an attorney:

- They have been practicing estate planning long enough to know what they are doing.
- They are referred by someone you trust, who knows the difference between a good and bad estate attorney.
- They are upfront about their costs. Otherwise, if you are just given an hourly rate, you may be writing a blank check.

- They keep documents current, as the laws and your situation change. We recommend an update of at least every three years.

Action Item: Select an attorney you trust and feel comfortable asking all of your questions. Don't be afraid to ask about costs.

SELECTING A POWER OF ATTORNEY

The person you select as your power of attorney must be responsible, because they will have to pay your bills as well as make medical decisions for you, if you are unable.

Consider a back-up if, heaven forbid, you get hurt and cannot pay your bills and your first choice cannot do it either. This person acts on your behalf.

Pick wisely and make sure they:

1. Have several copies of an original power of attorney document
2. Can get into your home or condo
3. Know where your mail, bills, checks and records are kept
4. Know your wishes and spending choices

As you get older, you might consider adding them to your checking account.

Make sure your power of attorney, your emergency contact at the hospital and your primary physician are called if you have an accident or are admitted to a hospital. If you have a pet or children, make sure your power of attorney knows who is to care for them if you cannot.

Many people have a plan for death, but not for disability. Create a plan for both and make sure your power of attorney knows where you keep the cash in your home and where you're current asset and debt listings are stored. If you have a safety deposit box, be sure they know where the box is located and where to find the key. If you have a special needs child, find an attorney who specializes in a special needs trust. If this is not set up properly, an inheritance can disqualify them from the much needed government assistance programs.

What Does Your Executor Need?

The executor needs the same list of documents as the person who is your power of attorney. He also will need a copy of your wills, trust and powers of attorneys, as well as key phone numbers of your banker, investment advisor, supervisor at work, insurance agent, attorney and tax advisor.

If you own a business, ensure your executor has access to key company documents – articles of incorporation, key company agreements and insurance.

Realize that, from the time the power of attorney ends at death and until the court appoints the executor, as much as four to six months may pass. Make sure the responsible party has access to enough money to pay basic bills, for at least six months or this could cause severe problems.

If you are receiving income, pensions or Social Security benefits, make sure they know who to contact to stop the payments.

And, if burial arrangements are not made in advance, make sure they know your desires as to where you want to be buried and how. We know this is morbid to think about, but unless you tell the people you trust what your wishes are, their job will be much harder to carry out.

Jerry had outlived everyone. His wife of 60 years died nine years before him. With no children, Jerry set up his estate to go to charity with a private foundation to make things go smoothly. His estate was worth well over $1 million dollars.

At 93, he was still driving himself around and doing fine.

Then Jerry came down with an infection. I was called to the hospital as his prognosis was given. They gave Jerry only a few months to live.

I had come to know and love Jerry over the past several years. Once or twice a month, I had breakfast with him. Also, it had become a tradition for Jerry to celebrate holidays with our family.

Now, his life was coming to an end and we made sure he was loved and with people who cared about him. He was always good spirited even in his final days. The end came peacefully on a Wednesday evening.

After he passed away, I helped to ensure his funeral went as he desired. He was buried with full military honors at Fort Snelling Cemetery. People came from all over to give tribute to him. Having his estate plan in place made things go as he wished.

Jerry's legacy is a foundation that will give to others in need for years to come.

Family Estate Meeting

We recommend having a family estate meeting. As a general rule, do not have your children's spouses present, as you will want to discuss how you plan to protect family money from outside threats including possible future ex-spouses.

Go over the plan to transfer assets to blood relatives, rather than stepchildren or replacement spouses.

In the meeting cover key issues like:

- Who is the executor?
- Who is the power of attorney?
- How will property get divided?
- Where are the records kept?
- Where do you wish to be buried and how?
- Medical wishes—who should be called if you are sick?
- What key people to contact if there is a problem?

- Which charities to receive donations on death
- Who will make copies of family photos and distribute them?
- How you intend to distribute assets?
- What people should be invited to your funeral and where to run notices?
- Who you use for tax, legal and investment advising?

Remember Lily? Because of trying the "do-it-yourself" estate plan, Lily ended up giving more of her assets to her ex-husband after the death of their son because of a poorly thought out do-it-yourself estate plan. Needless to say, her ex was thrilled. After she mentioned her past problems, we suggested she have her estate plan set up right.

She then hired an attorney who specialized in estate planning, and her sister and family are named as her executor and beneficiary.

Action Item: Write in your journal when you will have a family meeting, without your children's' spouses. Then go over your estate plan and suggest they do the same with their affairs.

SUMMARY

Estate planning is not something to be taken on by the untrained, no more than surgery or engineering.

1. Find an attorney to help you match up the right documents to your situation. Know costs in advance and then plan to keep documents current.

2. Make sure those who are designated as your powers of attorney and executors know where to find the things they need to do their jobs.

3. Have a family meeting so there are no surprises, which if not addressed, can divide families for a lifetime over a favorite picture album or wedding ring. The more you do now, the fewer problems your estate will cause after your death.

4. Write your wishes as to how and where you want to be buried and who should conduct the services.

5. Update your estate plan as your situation or net worth changes, or as estate planning laws change.

The best laid plans start with the end in mind. Once you know where you want to go, you simply work backwards until you are back to where you stand today. Then check the plan going forward and make sure the journey is possible.

VIII. CONCLUSION

We started this journey through these pages and since the beginning of the book we assembled a vision of how you want your life to be. You created a plan. We suggested that you use a journal to keep the plan relevant, alive and current.

Then, you came up with a plan to increase your income by increasing the value you provide to your employer, or by learning a higher paying profession so you deserve more income, bonus or salary.

We came up with ways to help all types of savers – those with *Great*, *Good* and *Poor* cash flows. Then, we had you identify ways to help increase your savings to a minimum of 10 percent. Once you have a minimum of 10 percent free cash flow, you can use it to retire your consumer debt in no more than four years and your mortgage in no more than 10 years.

With some investable income available, we address why most people who receive a windfall have it lost in no time at all. You learned what makes an asset an "investment" versus a non-performing asset. Then, you came up with ways to transform non-performing assets into investment assets to expand your portfolio.

We discovered why emotions drive the wrong behaviors in most investors. They typically buy high and sell low. We analyzed what makes a good investment. Specifically, we discussed why you should own investments that make money, have great cash flow, have a high re-investment rate, have high earnings growth potential, and are purchased at a bargain price.

You learned how to structure your holdings so you can practice "buying low" and "selling high." More accurately, you will buy, then wait a year and add to the sectors that are down while selling in the sectors that have moved up. We discussed the importance of balancing the investment portfolio in U.S. and overseas investments, as well as in income and growth investments.

You learned that all investment types must still pass the test of being an "investment." Then, we reviewed each basic type and why they are good and where the disadvantages lurk within each investment, so you can make a return after taxes and inflation.

We spent time on how to improve tax preparation and how to find a great accountant. Also we covered why it is important to start the tax work before the year is up to allow you to lower your tax proactively.

You learned how having a business can reduce your taxes. You learned that giving is a great way to help others and save on your taxes. You learned how much to add to your retirement account and why. You looked at converting ordinary income into dividends and long-term capital gains to significantly change your after tax portfolio returns. We addressed how to stop phantom income by minimizing mutual funds in non-retirement accounts. We briefly touched on planning for an audit.

Then, we inspected your financial boat for holes – risks that jeopardize your future. We covered long-term health care, life insurance, disability and other key insurance policy needs. We covered ways to insure some of your investment holdings. Then, we addressed issues surrounding the disposition of your estate – so your assets go to whom you want, while minimizing estate taxes.

Whew! That's a lot to cover. From beginning to end this book took me almost a year to write and refine. Hopefully, you find it helpful. There is a checklist in the back of the book to help you address each aspect of your finances. Thank you for taking the time to read these few pages. If you found this book helpful, let others know about it. If you need help, let us know. You can always reach us at www.brettmachtig.com.

So ask yourself, if you really took this material and addressed each issue in earnest, would it improve your income? Would it reduce your debt and other expenses? Would it increase your savings in investments that make money? Would your investments do better? Would your risks be fewer and your taxes lower? Would your estate be better addressed? If so this book is a success.

Our goal is to bring order to your finances. We hope this book accomplished that, as it will give you more control and more time to spend with those that matter most - your loved ones.

Have a prosperous journey, enjoy the ride!

conclusion

There is a danger in reading a book; It gives you ideas that, unless applied, only become frustrations. Once you take those ideas and apply them, they become wisdom – applied knowledge.

IX. FINANCIAL CHECKLIST

So now it's time to take all you learned and turn it into an action plan. As you review the important points in this book, use this checklist to make sure you address each aspect of your financial situation. For each task record a start date and the date the task is completed. Once done, monitor and track results quarterly as outlined on page 19.

I. **THE SECRET TO BEING FINANCIALLY STRESS-FREE RIGHT NOW**

	Task Started	Task Completed

- Buy a 5" x 8" journal and keep it with you so you can work on the plan, p. 20

    ___/___/___   ___/___/___

- Create 10-Year Vision, p. 21

    ___/___/___   ___/___/___

- Create five-Year Vision, p. 23

    ___/___/___   ___/___/___

	Task Started	Task Completed

- Create three-Year Vision, p. 24

  ___/___/___   ___/___/___

- Create one-Year Vision p. 26

  ___/___/___   ___/___/___

- List five things "to do right now…" p. 26

  ___/___/___   ___/___/___

- Create list of mentors who can help you, p. 28

  ___/___/___   ___/___/___

- Calculate Net Income Table, p. 190

  ___/___/___   ___/___/___

- Calculate Debt Payoff Table, p. 192

  ___/___/___   ___/___/___

- Calculate Expense Table, p. 194

  ___/___/___   ___/___/___

- Calculate Savings Table, p. 196

  ___/___/___   ___/___/___

II. THE SINGLE MOST IMPORTANT FACTOR TO FINANCIAL SUCCESS

	Task Started	Task Completed

- Classify your cash flow (great, good, or poor) and follow program to improve condition, p. 38

  __/__/__   __/__/__

- Generate ideas to increase income, p. 41

  __/__/__   __/__/__

- Create debt reduction plan, p. 42

  __/__/__   __/__/__

- Reduce business expenses, p. 42

  __/__/__   __/__/__

- Reduce child-related expenses, p. 43

  __/__/__   __/__/__

- Reduce vacation expenses, p. 44

  __/__/__   __/__/__

- Reduce insurance expenses, p. 44

  __/__/__   __/__/__

	Task Started	Task Completed

- Reduce home expenses, p. 45

  ___/___/___   ___/___/___

- Reduce toys & 2nd homes costs, p. 45

  ___/___/___   ___/___/___

- Reduce auto expenses, p. 46

  ___/___/___   ___/___/___

- Reduce unplanned expenses, p. 47

  ___/___/___   ___/___/___

- Reduce remodeling expenses, p. 47

  ___/___/___   ___/___/___

- Reduce real estate expenses, p. 48

  ___/___/___   ___/___/___

Add up total estimated savings based on what you are willing to change from each spending category. This number should be at least a 10% less than your net income on. p. 190

  ___/___/___   ___/___/___

III. FIVE KEYS TO HELP INCREASE YOUR INVESTING SUCCESS

	Task Started	Task Completed

- Investing – list your assets. Then identify if they are non-producing or investments? p. 56

  ___/___/___   ___/___/___

- List any non-producing assets you need to change, when and how. p. 63

  ___/___/___   ___/___/___

- List your investments; do they pass the tests of a great investment? (1) Do they make money? (2) Do they have great cash flow? (3) Do they have the potential to make a great return? If not, sell and replace with ones that pass the tests of a great investments. p. 68

  ___/___/___   ___/___/___

- Does your portfolio make money after taxes and inflation?

  p. 70

  ___/___/___   ___/___/___

- Did you buy at a bargain, sell when everyone wants it? Does everyone love or hate it? Hate is a good time to buy. Love is a good time to sell. p. 81

  ___/___/___   ___/___/___

IV. <u>THE ESSENTIALS TO EFFECTIVE DIVERSIFICATION</u>

Divide investments in these classes:

1. Cash/CD's p. 87 $_____

                                        ___%

2. Fixed Return/Guaranteed p. 88 $_____

                                        ___%

3. Bonds/Annuities p. 88-93 $_____

                                        ___%

4. Stocks p. 93-96 $_____

                                        ___%

5. Real Estate p. 96 $_____

                                        ___%

6. Non-correlated Investments p. 97 $_____

                                        ___%

    Total Investments $_____

                                        <u>100%</u>

	Task Started	Task Completed

- Have your assets passed the test of diversification? Am I over-concentrated? Am I buying high, selling low? Write an investment allocation plan. p. 99

  ___/___/___   ___/___/___

- Account types – have you set up separate income, expense, and savings, (investment) accounts? Do you pay yourself at least 10%, before income can enter an expense account? Do you have a system to know what you make, spend and save every month? Do you track your debt balance changes each month? p.103

  ___/___/___   ___/___/___

V. THE KEYS TO REAL INCOME TAX REDUCTION

	Task Started	Task Completed

- Buy TurboTax before year-end and estimate your taxes. Then run different tax scenarios to CHANGE your tax, based on what scenario is best for you. (p.125)

  ___/___/___   ___/___/___

- Find or keep a great accountant. (p.126)

  ___/___/___   ___/___/___

- Consider ideas for starting your own business, and how they could benefit you. (p. 132)

  ___/___/___   ___/___/___

- Review your retirement plan contributions. Should you increase them or decrease them and increase non-qualified savings? (p. 138)

  ___/___/___   ___/___/___

- Restructure your investments to significantly change your tax. (p. 140)

  ___/___/___   ___/___/___

- Be prepared for an audit. (p. 142)

  ___/___/___   ___/___/___

VI. <u>PROTECTING WHAT YOU HAVE</u>

	Date

Review the following insurance needs:

1. Long term health care, p. 150   ___/___/___

2. Life insurance, p. 154   ___/___/___

3. Disability insurance, p. 155   ___/___/___

4. Umbrella insurance, p. 155   ___/___/___

5. Health insurance, p. 156   ___/___/___

6. Home insurance, p. 156   ___/___/___

7. Auto insurance, p. 157   ___/___/___

Reduce insurance costs. Write plan to:

    Improve health   ___/___/___

    Adjust deductibles   ___/___/___

    Anticipate estate taxes   ___/___/___

VII. <u>ESTATE PLANNING MADE SIMPLE</u>

	Task Started	Task Completed

- Review your estate needs, p. 163

       __/__/__   __/__/__

- Create key documents, p. 166

       __/__/__   __/__/__

- Select an Attorney, Executors and POAs, p. 167

       __/__/__   __/__/__

- Have a family meeting, p. 170

       __/__/__   __/__/__

VIII. CONCLUSION

	Task Started	Task Completed

- Let us know if you would be interested in attending a workshop in your city.

  ___/___/___   ___/___/___

- Let us know if you need help in finding an attorney, identity theft protection, an insurance agent or a financial advisor in your area.

  ___/___/___   ___/___/___

- Let us know how this book helped and if you need help by contacting us at www.brettmachtig.com or by calling 952-831-8243.

  ___/___/___   ___/___/___

Practice makes perfect. Model successful actions.

X. FINANCIAL PLAN EXAMPLE

Bob and Mary are your typical yuppie couple from Telluride, Colo. Bob works in the telecom industry and Mary stays home with their kids. Bob has a great job and made it through the telecom woes of the early 2000s without losing his job. He did, however, lose a great deal of money, via the stock bubble of 2000 and the meltdown of MCI.

Bob and Mary have their eyes set on preparing for retirement. They have a rental property worth $300,000, down from its peak price of $350,000 a few years ago. They receive rent of $900 per month, but also have a $200,000 mortgage, on which they pay $2,000 per month. They have a loan balance on a retail furniture credit card and $16,000 in credit balances from remodeling their rental property. They also have monthly payments associated with the property totaling $2,750. Each month the rental property creates $1,850 in negative cash flow.

They have a good income, but each month the couple can barely keep their heads above water. After an initial consultation, we put together a plan for Bob and Mary. After taxes and adding in returns on their $250,000 retirement portfolio, they just break even.

Action Item: Use the table on the opposing page as an example of how to calculate your net income.

We crafted Bob & Mary's plan by first concentrating on their net income. Because of his job and industry, Bob can only expect to get three percent inflationary wage increases.

The next page shows a sample table* we used to compute Bob and Mary's net income:

Year	Gross Pay	Bus./ Real Estate Income	Invest. Income (8% Return)	Income Taxes	Net Income
Now	130k	11k	20k	(-15k)	146k
Y1	130k	11k	20k	(-19k)	142k
Y2	134k	5k	120k	(-20k)	239k
Y3	139k		18k	(-21k)	136k
Y4	144k		18k	(-22k)	140k
Y5	149k		22k	(-22k)	149k
Y6	154k		29k	(-23k)	160k
Y7	160k		38k	(-24k)	174k
Y8	165k		47k	(-25k)	187k
Y9	171k		57k	(-26k)	202k
Y10	177k		67k	(-26k)	218k

*Rounded to the nearest thousand. This example is hypothetical and does not represent any specific securities product and/or insurance policy. Actual results will vary. This is for information purposes only. You should consult with your attorney and accountant for legal and tax advice. Please visit www.brettmachtig.com to download a free cash flow analysis template.

HOW TO USE THE TABLE: (1) Put in earned income including wages, pensions and Social Security. Do not include small business income, investment real estate and investment income as they have their own columns. (2) Put any rental property or small business income here. (3) Use your best estimate of return on your investments. (4) Include estimate of income tax. (5) Put in other gross income deductions like 401(k) contributions here. (6) Add incomes and subtract taxes and deductions to calculate your net income.

What is your gross W-2 income? What is your real estate or small business income? What do you estimate the returns from your investments? What do you expect from your taxes and deductions? As you read this book, ask yourself, "What is my net income?" "What do I get to actually spend?" Use this example to figure out how to calculate what your net income will be for the next 10 years.

Expenses

Expenses are everything you spend money on to live your life, excluding savings. It didn't take an accounting degree for Bob and Mary to quickly realize that they would never be able to improve their cash flow without addressing their debt, which constituted $75,960 of expenses to their $130,960 in net income.

In other words, debt payments translated to 58 percent of all their expenses.

> Action Item: Use the Table on the opposing page as an example of how to calculate your debt.

Here is Bob and Mary's debt table*:

Name	Debt Balance	Interest Rate	Payment	Total Ann. Exp.
Mortgage	250k	6%	2.5k	30k
GM '05	15k	6%	.4k	5k
Ford F150 '07	25k	6%	.3k	4k
Invest. Property	200k	7%	2k	24k
2nd Mortgage	27k	8%	.2k	2.5k
VISA	10k	15%	.3k	4k
Furniture Loan	5k	19%	.5k	6k
Mastercard	11k	21%	.3k	4k
Total	$543k	6%	6.5k	80k

*Rounded to the nearest thousand. This example is hypothetical and does not represent any specific securities product and/or insurance policy. Actual results will vary. This is for information purposes only. You should consult with your attorney and accountant for legal and tax advice. Please visit www.brettmachtig.com to download a free cash flow analysis template. Please visit www.brettmachtig.com to download free cash flow analysis template

HOW TO USE THE TABLE: (1) Put in remaining debt balance. (2) Put in current interest rate. (3) Put in your debt payments, principle and interest, excluding mortgage withholdings. (4) Put in annual debt payments.

Bob and Mary's Debt-Payoff Plan

Bob and Mary fell into the same trap that catches many real estate investors – poor cash flow. They listed and sold their rental property at a loss. By using the proceeds from the investment property equity they improved their cash flow. They went from owing $543,000 to being 100-percent debt-free in 40 months! They reduced their personal expenses by 58 percent without any reduction in lifestyle whatsoever in about three years. By adding $500 extra to the highest interest debt payment monthly and selling their investment property, Bob and Mary used property sale proceeds to pay off debt.

This debt pay-off plan reduced their expenses by 58 percent in 40 months without a change in lifestyle.

This is one of the simplest debt management strategies, and one that worked for Bob and Mary.

Pay off the highest interest item, and then put the paid-off payment amount towards the next highest item on the debt list until that debt is paid off. Continue adding the payment of retired debts to the next highest interest bearing debt item. With any windfalls or bonuses, put at least half toward debt retirement.

Bob and Mary's planned expenses include a new car for $30,000 in Year 2, home remodeling in Year 4, and paying $10,000 annually for their son's college expenses.

Action Item: Use the Table on the opposing page as an example of how to calculate your expenses.

Here is a sample table* we used to compute Bob and Mary's expenses:

Year	Planned Exp.	Bus./Real Estate Exp.	Planned Exp.	Total Debt Payments	Planned Debt Payoff	Total Exp.
Now	48k	7k		76k	6k	137k
Y1	49k	7k		30k	52k	138k
Y2	51k		30k	30k	152k	262k
Y3	52k			30k	52k	134k
Y4	54k		15k	10k	17k	96k
Y5	56k					55k
Y6	57k					57k
Y7	59k		10k			69k
Y8	61k		10k			71k
Y9	62k		10k			72k
Y10	64k		10k			74k

*This example is hypothetical and does not represent any specific securities product and/or insurance policy. Actual results will vary. This is for information purposes only. You should consult with your attorney and accountant for legal and tax advice. Please visit www.brettmachtig.com to download free cash flow analysis template

HOW TO USE THE TABLE: (1) Put in monthly and periodic expenses that do not have a specific column above. (2) Put in business or investment real estate expenses. (3) Put in planned purchases like cars, remodeling, college expenses, second home, etc. (4) Put in debt payments you make now (5) Put in extra money here to pay off your consumer debt within 4 years and 10 years for your mortgage (6) Add across the columns, to get your total expenses.

Expenses are not just your planned expenses – they include everything you spend your money on. Include the following in your expense listing:

- Cash expenses

- Regular bills
- Insurance premiums
- Property taxes
- New cars
- Home upgrades
- Vacations
- Gifts to loved ones
- Repairs
- Unplanned purchases

Estimate your expenses for at least 10 years into the future. And, remember to make allowances for those random and unplanned expenses. Now that you know your net income, debt and total expenses, you can use this information to calculate your annual savings and portfolio growth.

Action Item: Use table on the opposing page as an example below of how to calculate your annual savings and portfolio growth.

Here is a sample savings table* we used to compute Bob and Mary's asset growth:

Year	Net Income	Total Expenses	Savings/ (Debt)	IRAs, 403(b)s, 401(k)s	Total Savings	Investment Portfolio
Now	140k	137k	3.8k	9k	135k	263k
Y1	146k	138k	7.6k	9k	172k	280k
Y2	253k	262k	(9.8)k	10k	141k	280k
Y3	169k	134k	34k	10k	448k	325k
Y4	183k	96k	87k	11k	98k	423k
Y5	199k	55k	144k	11k	155k	578k
Y6	216k	57k	159k	11k	170k	749k
Y7	234k	69k	165k	12k	177k	926k
Y8	254k	71k	183k	12k	195k	1,121k

*IN THOUSANDS. This example is hypothetical and does not represent any specific securities product and/or insurance policy. Actual results will vary. This is for information purposes only. You should consult with your attorney and accountant for legal and tax advice. Please visit www.brettmachtig.com to download free cash flow analysis template

HOW TO USE THE TABLE: (1) Copy net income from Net Income Table. (2) Copy total expenses from Expenses Table. (3) Subtract expenses from net income to get Savings or (Debt Creation). (4) Add up all retirement contributions. (5) Add Column 3 to Column 4 to get total savings. (6) Add the previous year's portfolio balance to current year's total savings to get the new investment portfolio balance.

If you need help in calculating income, expenses, savings and debt structure don't panic. A professional financial advisor can help you through these first steps.

As you can see in the savings table, by focusing on paying off debt, Bob and Mary's expenses dropped from $136,960 to $55,645 in 40 months. This change increased their savings, and at an assumed eight percent rate of return, their portfolio can cover their expenses within eight years (For illustration only, results not guaranteed).

Use the example to calculate your savings and portfolio growth. If your savings is less than 10 percent of your net income, ask yourself what you can do to reduce your five largest bills. The goal is to save at least 10 percent after all expenses, not including the retirement account savings.

An easy way to verify what you spend is to take your net income and subtract your past annual savings. Periodically add up your savings (including your liquid investments) and subtract your debt balances. If your debt went up and/or savings went down, then your expenses are more than your net income. This is bad. You need to address the poor cash flow.

financial plan example

XI. GLOSSARY

AB Trust: A legal document designed to split up your assets for estate planning purposes to double your estate tax exemptions.

Annuity: There are three basic types of annuities: fixed, indexed and variable. These are tax-deferred investments that insure the asset or income stream or provide a death benefit.

Asset: An asset is something you own of value. A car, a house, a college education, a business, an investment property, a doll collection, a cabin, cash, IRAs, 401(k), brokerage account, and your wedding ring all meet that broad definition. For purposes of this book, an asset is something you own that you can sell for money. There are two types – "investments" which can pay you money and "non-performing assets" which cost you money.

Asset Allocation: How a portfolio is divided among different types of investments, usually stock, bonds and cash. The goal of asset allocation is achieving the highest return possible without taking on more risk than the investor is comfortable.

Balanced Portfolio: A balanced portfolio contains roughly equal amounts of stocks and bonds.

Bear Market: A period of time during which stock prices are declining.

Beta: A measure of a stock's movement relative to the market. If a stock moves more than the market, it carries a beta greater than 1; if it moves less than the market, its beta is less than 1.

Bond: A debt security representing a contractual agreement by a company or government to repay borrowed money by a specified time at a specified rate.

Bull Market: A period of time during which stock prices are rising.

Buy-Sell Agreement: This is an agreement that spells out what each business partner will receive if a partner becomes disabled, leaves or dies.

Capital Appreciation: Increase in the price of an investment.

Capital Gain/Loss: The profit (or loss) that results from a change in the price of an asset. A realized gain (or loss) occurs when an investment security is sold at a price above (or below) its purchase price.

Capital Market: A broad term encompassing all the securities markets in which stocks, bonds and money market instruments are traded.

Capital Preservation: An investment objective in which protecting the investor's initial investment from loss is the primary goal.

Cash Equivalent: Cash Equivalent Investments are in short-term debt obligations issued by governments, banks and corporations that mature less than one year from issuance.

Cash Flow: Cash flow is cash received minus cash payments over a specified period of time. Ideal cash flow is having enough non-retirement savings so you can live from your portfolio within a reasonable time. For the purposes of this book, ideal minimum cash flow is at least 10 percent of funds that are free to use, save or pay-off debt after paying all expenses. We define GREAT cash flow as saving 50 percent or more of every dollar you make in net income. We define GOOD cash flow as saving 10 to 50 percent of net income. We define POOR cash flow as saving less than 10 percent of your net income.

Closed-End Mutual Fund: A mutual fund that offers a fixed number of shares for sale and trades on a stock exchange.

Commercial Paper: Unsecured debt generally issued by companies to meet short-term financing needs. Commercial paper represents a large portion of the money market.

Common Stock: Security representing ownership interest in a company. Common stock shares typically trade on the NYSE, NASDAQ, or the American Exchanges. Some also trade of foreign exchanges as well as ADRS on U.S. exchanges.

Consumer Price Index (CPI): A common measure of inflation. The CPI is equal to the sum of prices of a number of goods purchased by consumers and weighted by the proportion each represents in a typical consumers' budget.

Contrarian: An investor who purposely does the opposite of what most investors are doing. A contrarian investor tries to select securities that are out of favor with the market.

Credit Quality: Credit quality is a measure of the likelihood that a company will be able to make interest and principal payments on its bonds or other debt securities. Standard and Poor's Corporation and Moody' Investor Service rate the credit quality of publicly traded debt securities.

Direct Investments: Direct investments are investments made directly to the equity of items such as non-traded real estate investment trusts (REITS), direct oil and gas limited partnerships, leasing opportunities and Tenants In Common private transactions. These investments can offer good return, but with a very low correlation to either publicly-traded stocks, bonds, or other real estate. These are considered long-term investments and should be undertaken only by those investors who can afford to lose all the money invested.

Diversification: The process of investing in different types of investment classes to reduce the risk of poor performance by any one type of investment having a big impact on overall portfolio results. Our test of good diversification – your assets do not increase or decrease in value together.

Dividend: A cash payment made by a company to stockholders.

Dividend Yield: The total amount of cash dividend received annually on a share of stock divided by the stock price.

Durable Power of Attorney (POA): A revocable power granted for another to act on their behalf. Durable refers to the fact the power of attorney survives the "competence" of the individual. The power goes away if the person dies.

EAFE Index: An abbreviation for the Morgan Stanley index of overseas stock performance: Europe, Australia and Far East Index.

EPS or Earnings Per Share: A company's net income divided by the total number of outstanding shares. EPS is generally regarded as a measure of a firm's profitability.

Equity: The ownership interest of common and preferred stockholders in a company.

Equity-Indexed Annuities: Allow stock market participation with no down-side risk. The disadvantages are lack of liquidity, low returns and limited flexibility.

Expected Return: The expected return is the return investors anticipate they will receive on an investment over some future period. The expected return is often unrealistically higher than the investors' actual realized return.

Expenses: Expenses are everything you spend your money on. Expenses include cash expenses, regular monthly bills, quarterly bills, insurance premiums, holiday gifts, property taxes, new cars, home upgrades, vacations, gifts to loved ones, repairs and unplanned purchases.

Executor: The court-appointed personal representative who is authorized to settle an estate on behalf of the decedent.

Family Limited Partnership: An estate planning vehicle to transfer ownership to family members over time, while still maintaining control.

Financial Goals: The goals investors would like to achieve with their investments such as saving for retirement, funding educational expenses, paying for a major purchase in the future, etc.

Fixed Annuities: An annuity type that generally pays a fixed rate over a specific time, much like a CD, except they are not FDIC insured. When you consider these investments, make sure the guaranteed interest rate is for the same period as the withdrawal penalties.

Fixed Income Investments: Investments are debt securities, such as bonds and money market instruments, with specified interest and principal payment dates and amounts.

Foundations: Foundations, or more specifically, Private Charitable Foundations are legal entities that allow the transfer of gifts directly to charities. Once in place, these entities can continue to give long after a person dies.

Growth Stocks: Stocks of companies whose earnings are expected to grow rapidly. Growth stocks are publically-traded companies that pay investors by growing the value of the stock rather than from dividends.

Income: Income includes all money you make including your wages, pensions, social security payments, alimony, as well as other income paid from other sources.

Income Stocks: For the purposes of this book, income stocks are stocks that trade on the major exchanges and pay a minimum of 4 percent in dividends per year.

Insurance: The spreading out of risk so that by making a small payment a person can reduce the risk in a particular area. For example, Life, Health, Auto, and Home Insurance protect the insured from losses affecting specified risks.

Insurance Trust (ILIT Trust): An irrevocable trust that allows the funding of insurance outside of an estate. This vehicle can save a large estate a fortune.

Investment: Investments are defined for purposes of this book as assets that can pay you money. Good investments earn income, have good cash flow, have good earnings growth potential, and are purchased at a bargain price.

Investment Objective: The investment goal of an individual investor or portfolio manager. Objectives could be designed to general income, capital appreciation, or a blend of both.

Investment Portfolio: The combined securities held by an investor, no matter where they are held.

Irrevocable Trusts: A type of trust that cannot be changed once they are created.

Journal: A little book to write your vision, plans, and action items. This is highly recommended for writing down your vision, plans and goals.

Liquidity: The ease with which investments can be bought or sold quickly without having a major impact on their price.

Living Will and Health Care Directive: These are documents that specify who can act on your behalf in making health related decisions. These documents commonly define what precautions can be taken to keep you alive and your preferences regarding organ donation.

Long-term Healthcare Insurance: This insurance covers some of the costs of nursing homes and in some cases in-home health care.

Market Capitalization: Market capitalization is the market value of a company. It equals the current stock price multiplied by the total number of stock shares outstanding.

Market Timing: Attempting to sell investments before they decrease in value and buy when they are about to increase in value.

Money Market: The market in which short-term, highly liquid, low-risk assets such as Treasury bills, bank certificates of deposits (CDs), corporate commercial paper, and banker's acceptance notes are traded.

Mutual Fund: An investment fund that pools the money of many individuals and invests it on their behalf in accordance with predetermined investment objectives.

Net Income: For the purposes of this book, your personal next income is your earned income less payroll deductions and income taxes.

Nominal Return: The return on an investment, not adjusted for the effect of inflation.

Non-performing Assets: Assets which cost you money to support.

Open-End Mutual Fund: A mutual fund that stands ready to issue and redeem share of the fund as supply and demand dictate.

Ordinary Income: This is the income taxed at the highest personal rate on a federal basis. Its rate goes up depending on your income based upon the IRS Guidelines.

P/E Ratio or Price Earnings Ratio: The stock price divided by the earnings per share (EPS). It is the most often quoted measure of stock valuation.

Performance: The change in the value of a portfolio over a specific period of time. The overall performance of an investment includes income and capital gains or losses.

Phantom Income Taxes: These are tax liabilities incurred, even though an investment might not have earned that income while an investor owned the security. Mutual funds outside of retirement accounts can create this tax.

Plan: A written financial road map that shows where you have been, where you are and where you are going. Keep this in your journal and update it frequently in order to keep financially on track.

Portfolio Manager: The individual or firm responsible for the day-to-day decisions involving an investment portfolio. The manager decides which stocks or bonds to buy or sell and when.

Principal: The original amount invested in a security or portfolio.

Proactive Tax Planning: This is working to change your tax by changing your behavior before the year is over. For example, you can add to your retirement by making a donation or starting a business. If your income is very low you can chose to take money out of a retirement account and use the proceeds to improve cash flow.

Real Estate: Real estate might be a rental property, a commercial building, a REIT or a private placement.

Real Estate Investment Trust (REIT): A company that manages a portfolio of real estate properties.

Real Return: The return on an investment minus the effects of inflation. The goal is for you to make a positive return after taxes and inflation.

Risk: The possibility that the actual return on an investment will be different from the expected return. In general, the greater the risk, the greater the possible return on an investment.

Risk-Free Investment: An investment that has absolute certainty you will receive a specified return after a specified period of time. Although there are truly no risk-free investments, U.S. Treasury securities are considered risk-free investments.

Revocable Trusts: A type of trust that can be changed at any time, up to an executing event, like dying.

S&P 500, or Standard and Poor's 500: A Market value index of the stock market that is used to measure stock market activity. It measures the performance of 500 large public companies' common stocks and is often used as a proxy for the stock market.

Securities and Exchange Commission (SEC): A federal government agency, which was created by Securities and Exchange Act of 1934 that regulates the securities industry and administers federal securities laws.

Stocks: See common stocks and equity.

Time Horizon: The time investors allow to reach their asset growth of their investments.

Total Return: The total amount a given investment returns to investors, including any capital gains or losses and stock dividends or interest from interest bearing securities.

UGMA: Universal Gift to Minors Act is a law enacted to provide a simple way to transfer cash and securities to a minor without the complication of a formal trust and without the restrictions applicable to the guardianship of a minor's property.

Umbrella Policy: A type of insurance policy that covers the gap in your homeowners insurance and auto insurance policies, and also increases the upper limits of these two policies.

Unit Investment Trust (UIT): A professionally selected, then essentially unmanaged portfolio of securities.

UTMA: Universal Transfer To Minors Act extends the definition of gifts beyond cash and securities to include real estate, paintings, royalties, and patents. Prohibits minor from taking control of assets until age 21 (25 in California).

Value Stocks: Stocks that are traded at a cheap price relative to the company's perceived worth.

Variable Annuities: A type of annuity that offers a guaranteed death benefit and variable income and asset guarantees.

Vision: For this book, vision is where you want to be in 10 years in as vivid of detail as you can paint. Once the 10-year vision is clear, a five year vision can be written, followed by a three year and one year vision. Lastly, you can define what six things you need to do right now to be on track for your one-year vision. Write your answers in your journal.

Volatility: The degree to which a portfolio's value increases or decreases.

Wealth: For this book wealth is defined as the state or condition of being able to live off of the income generated by your investment portfolio.

Will: A legal document that specifies your wishes of how your assets are to be distributed upon your death.

XII. ACKNOWLEDGMENTS

First, I would like to thank the many clients who have let me into their lives. It is hard to consider what I do as work, because most of my time is spent visiting with friends and clients, helping solve financial problems, or studying investments.

Second, I would like to thank the colleagues who helped with this book project. I would also like to thank Lois Reuter, Mike Havlik, Cole Peyton, and Terri Simon, who have all helped make the book an easy read.

Third, I'd like to thank my fellow advisors who helped with content. Specifically, Michael Dmowski, Jim Chase, Jim DuPont, Dave Denniston, Jim Swirtz, and Mark Foreman. Each advisor added content and insight—boiling down material from their unique perspectives.

Fourth, I'd like to thank Ted Charles, Tim Murphy, Bill Atherton, Don Ingram, Ellis Liddell and John Hollosy for the support they offered as peers and from the home office at Investors Capital Corporation.

Fifth, I'd like to thank my wife, Nikki and my wonderful children – Jonathan, Ashley and Abby for the time they gave up with me so I could finish this book.

Sixth, I would like to thank our Heavenly Father for his divine inspiration.